Best Wishes!
Harvey J Coleman

Empowering Yourself

The Organizational Game Revealed

SECOND EDITION

Harvey J. Coleman

Coleman Management Consultants, Inc.

KENDALL/HUNT PUBLISHING COMPANY
4050 Westmark Drive Dubuque, Iowa 52002

Contents

CHAPTER FOUR

CHAPTER FIVE

CHAPTER SIX

CHAPTER SEVEN

CHAPTER EIGHT

CHAPTER NINE

CHAPTER TEN

Acknowledgments

If the game of life is about people, I have been truly blessed, thanks to the great start in life I was given by my parents, Harry and Dollie Coleman. Thanks to the support I have received along the way from my family, Paquita, Kevin, Keith, and Kellie, and a special thanks to Alberta Lloyd who, for the last twenty-nine years, has helped me better understand what this game is all about.

Also, to all of my friends and my associates at Coleman Management Consultants who have been so supportive, I couldn't have done it without you. Thanks all!

Preface

My experience with the corporate world probably parallels that of many others in organizations. The successes I've enjoyed are easily explained by ambition and hard work. But I can also lay claim to a blockbuster defeat that transformed me from an optimistic young executive to a disenchanted skeptic. This crisis prompted my resignation from the IBM Corporation. This move subsequently led to the formation of Coleman Management Consultants, Inc.

During the decade following my departure from big business, through countless seminars and speaking engagements, I heard thousands of stories similar to my own. Some employees are on an apparent fast track to the presidency when suddenly, for no discernible reason, they find themselves passed over for promotion. Of course, many people handle career defeats in ways more creative than resigning. They may coast into retirement or hold daily complaint sessions around the water cooler.

Tragically, these unhappy people are sending up a massive wail from every type of occupation, from the naval yards of Virginia to the vineyards of California, from the boardrooms in Chicago to the drilling rigs in the Gulf. Ask them, and not one person can tell you how they wound up in their predicament or how they will escape it.

This book is for the frustrated. It is for a nation of employees frozen in place like so many victims of Pompeii. It is also for those who are currently advancing their careers without recognizing defeat lurking ahead. Be careful. Many are bumped from the ladder at the uppermost rungs—a phenomenon today referred to as hitting the "glass ceiling."

This book is for the soldier whose ultimate goal is to work at the Pentagon, the government employee who wishes to rise high in the Senior Executive Service (SES) ranks, and the student who has a grasp of the technical challenge but is unclear as to the application of "the softer skills." From educator to administrator, anyone who has to maneuver a hierarchy to achieve his or her ultimate goals, this book is for you.

This book is also for the wife or husband who sees uncomfortable activity around the house, activity that requires one's own participation. If you're the spouse who is asked to take up bridge or tennis, there just might be a legitimate reason behind that request. I trust this book will help you understand what your partner is doing, although it may be a burden to appreciate it fully.

And this book is even for the few happy souls among us, those who are intuitively doing everything right. Curious about your charmed path to the top? Want to know why your route to the presidency has been lined with rose petals and admiring crowds?

Herein are chapters that suggest life is a game, not at all a trivial one, but a game nonetheless. This is a game about people and their reactions. All else is just the chatter of detail. Further, this game of life is governed by rules, with the most important rules being ones that are unwritten and that apply not only to the business culture but almost every organizational culture as well.

My purpose in writing this book is to expose the rules of your game . . . whether you're in business, education, the military, civil service, or a non-profit organization. The rules apply to them all. Once we know the rules, life then becomes a series of thoughtful moves and countermoves rather than a series of bold reactions to haphazard bombshells lobbed our way.

When you know the rules, success comes to those most adept at playing.

Welcome to the game!

CHAPTER 1

The People Game

It was my understanding that the path to senior-level management and to the executive suite lay solely in hard work. After all, family and friends alike, even my college professors, had ushered me into the business world with a parting battle cry. "Work hard," they said, "and you'll go far."

At first, the well-intended advice seemed filled with merit. After a successful sales stint at Xerox, I stepped onto the fast track at IBM as a young executive headed for the top. One evening, I afforded myself a rare moment to reflect on my work history. It had been filled with long hours, with total commitment to my career, and I was rewarded with a steady stream of promotions.

That evening, amid the clutter of pie charts and business plans, I reasoned that career advancement is the obvious result of hard work. Therefore, because I had no aversion to working hard, I should be the company's CEO in a few years. On the spot, I proposed my philosophy. "I'll give one hundred percent, exert every effort, accept any task, and the company will promote me according to my proven results." That's what I thought the company was telling me, and that's what I believed. Even now, as I look back, it seems like a contract of fairness and equality.

But you're probably ahead of me already. Rule number one in the system's culture insists: "Nobody said it was going to be fair!"

For if hard work is all it takes to excel at one's career, if our advancement is based strictly on results, then how are promotions made when several able managers rise simultaneously toward a single position? I knew of several others in my department who worked nights, weekends, and holidays. What would distinguish one of us from the other?

It was a question I had never considered and one whose answer proved my downfall.

How Can They Do This?

I never really questioned the process of candidate selection until my seventh year on the job at IBM, and then I questioned it a great deal. I held a fairly visible position in the company, one where my results were easily compared with eleven other managers throughout the nation. The results I was posting at the time put me in a secure third place, which wasn't bad considering the caliber of the competition. So I wasn't surprised when the two ahead of me were promoted. I was *very* surprised, however, when the fourth-ranked manager was also promoted.

My manager saw me that afternoon, at my request. Foregoing pleasantries, I bluntly asked why I had been passed over. He responded with a non-answer. "Just keep working hard," he said. "Don't worry about it."

Work hard? Don't worry about it? I was *already* working hard. And I was going to worry. For the first time in my career, I had been passed over for promotion, and I was being asked to treat it like a broken shoelace. I didn't have the slightest clue why I had been passed over, and my manager, the only person who could give me a definitive answer, had just passed the whole matter off with a yawn!

That year, I went on to top every objective measurement for my job title. My peers fell away below me, into a distant second, third, fourth place, and on into the haze. I had done all I could do. True to my philosophy, I had worked very hard. My results proved it, and I was ready for the pay-off. That pay-off was indeed delivered—to two others far down in the standings. Once more, I went back to my boss, asking for help. He shrugged. "You have to be patient," he said. "It'll happen."

Perhaps. But maybe it would *not* happen. I felt my motivation drop a few notches as confusion seeped in. I had given them my best, yet I wasn't receiving any guidance on how to overcome this rock-solid barrier that had stopped my advancement so suddenly.

Six months later, I was passed over a third time despite my continued high standings. I was caught on some sort of treadmill that kept slamming me against the invisible barrier, and the bruises tore away at my work philosophy. There I stood, with my top-notch results on every manager's desk all the way up the line, and yet I was absolutely, undeniably unpromotable. And it hurt.

Thoroughly disgusted, I drew the only conclusion I could understand at that time in my life. The game was rigged. Good ol' Mother Liberty, with her huddled masses and confounded executives, had torched my work ethic.

Powerless to control my own destiny, and apparently the victim of some high-level crap shoot, I resigned, bursting with hefty amounts of resentment, anger, confusion, and a deep feeling of betrayal by a system that had turned its back on the private contract I believed in so strongly. The one I had never told anyone about, but the one which was so sensible: "Hard work and results are rewarded by promotion."

Ready . . . Set . . . Crash!

It hurt when I hit that barrier. I was moving very fast, and the impact left me bitter. The faster anyone moves in a career, the harder a person tries, the more it hurts when the goal is missed.

To some extent, every employee in the nation is working, just as I was, with a secret contract locked away in the desk drawer. And they might be setting themselves up for a bitter encounter with the same ceiling I met. Their contract might not say exactly what mine did, but these contracts shape career decisions, and expectations, coast to coast.

The problem is, most work philosophies are constructed in a manner which allows the wounded employee to shift blame to the company whenever an apparent injustice has occurred. Mine was like that. I honestly felt that my company was to blame when my results, according to my evaluation and philosophy, meant that I should be promoted and was not. It never occurred to me that I could control my future. However, with my limited knowledge of *the game* and my limited actions on the job, I hadn't allowed the company a choice, other than to pass me over.

You Really Are in Control

You are in charge of your destiny! It's time to kill all the scapegoats and confront that image in the mirror. You can accomplish anything in your career as long as you understand and accept some major ground rules of the game. You see, your career, and life in general, is a part of the game, but the ingredient that makes it all work is people. Yes, that's right, the game is about people. Everything else in life is just detail. *Everything* else is detail.

This includes your focus on advancing your career and your quest for riches. Career advancement and money may well be in your future, but *only* when you first take care of the people who touch your life. Money is just a by-product of your relationship with people. Impress the boss, and you get the pay raise. You will never, ever, receive a promotion unless another person agrees to it. That's why I say you're in charge of your own destiny. You are the only person who can control your interaction with people around you.

Since life is about people, since your *job* is among, for, and about people, and since you control your interaction with people, then you have full control to take yourself anywhere you want to go. You, in fact, *are* the boss.

But First . . . !

Just one thing. In order for us to have a true shot at the top, which means bypassing that career-jolting ceiling I hit, all of us need to leave from the same starting gate. Many of us have worked for years with a heavy anchor that we didn't even realize we were dragging. Even though we might have worked harder than anyone else in the company, we were probably never in the race for upper management. We didn't understand the game.

Life's game is played out on a game board shaped like a pyramid.

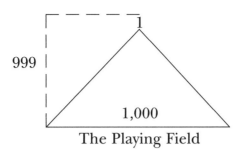

The Playing Field

Notice how it comes to a point at the top. The shape means anyone entering at the bottom in a company of 1,000 employees must outdistance 999 others if the goal is to be CEO. Now, when *every* employee knows the secret of reaching that peak, the game shifts onto a more equitable playing field, one which assures all candidates an equal opportunity for promotion, based on the quality of play.

When the rules of the game become common knowledge to everyone, this is a rare business situation where everyone wins. Employees win because they know the choices they must make to have an opportunity to reach the top. Thus, more employees will participate fully in their work when they understand how promotions are made. The company also wins when motivated employees improve productivity and quality.

I've taken some liberties in calling your career a game, although it should be noted that it is a serious one. I do feel there is justification in referring to the organizational world as a game, and it might even be enjoyable to approach it as such.

First, for a game to exist, there must be a contest or some sort of struggle. This is an obvious match. Without too much effort, you can probably recount a recent work situation that was difficult or seemingly impossible to resolve. In careers there are constant challenges, between you and your customers, your employees, your managers, your co-workers, your work, or between you and the system itself.

A game also engages opposing interests, which means you must have competition. The organizational game is certainly competitive! Wherever you are on the pyramid game board, you can safely assume that you and many of your co-workers want the same job. You definitely have competition. Players most adept at handling this competition will eventually reach the upper portion of the pyramid.

Competition may take different forms. One form is the individual competition that I faced. Everyone in my office competed for the same vacancy. Ideally, we like for this type of competition to be a friendly rivalry. This can be achieved, but only if everyone knows and plays by the same rules. Otherwise, the game will be viewed as unfair to the other players . . . and they'll resent the handicap. In the new team environments within many organizations, rewards will be given to those players that compete by making contributions without hurting other teammates or hindering the spirit of cooperation, which is essential.

This type of friendly and yet supportive competition can be seen at any National Basketball Association (NBA) game. Simply watch the players on any team sitting on the bench during the last two minutes of play. Almost every player on the bench wishes he could be in the action during the closing seconds, and some of the sidelined players believe they belong in the game. Despite these feelings, all will erupt from the bench to their feet when any of their teammates make a decisive play, which takes the team closer to victory. They, in fact, become the most enthusiastic and supportive individuals in the entire arena. However, during the next week of practice, those same players will do all they can in their play to replace one of the starters.

The other type of competition is inter-company, Ford versus General Motors, Boeing versus McDonnell Douglas, DEC versus IBM. There's a robust rivalry in this arena, extending into the international marketplace where the U.S. competes with Japan, and where Japan competes with Korea. Just as the most skillful individual wins the game at a specific level, so do the more able companies and nations emerge foremost among their competitors. The simple fact is that without competition we would never achieve the excellence needed to produce winning results.

Next, in order for this to be a true game, there must be specific information or guidelines available; in other words, you must have rules. You wouldn't think of playing a new card game without asking for rules. Neither would you coach a football team without giving the players the "Game Book." Yet, we're engaged in a very serious game without being aware of some of the more important rules. One of the truths of any game is that people who do not know the rules of the game they are playing, no matter how much they want to win or how hard they try, will not do very well. In order to win, they need the rules.

Finally, as in any game, if true empowerment is to exist, everyone must be allowed a *choice of moves*. Our decisions about our careers, and the things we're willing to trade off in exchange for the ability to accomplish our goals, become a direct barometer of our potential for success.

Choice? It's Your Move

Every game player understands the importance of *choice*. A series of well planned, well executed moves drives any player closer to success. But at the same time, one serious miscalculation can sidetrack a career.

The organizational game involves a series of increasingly difficult choices that come in the form of trade-offs. These trade-offs sometime help us to *choose* to plateau our career. Many of us, for example, wouldn't want to be president of the United States. The pressures, lack of privacy, and life-and-death decisions of the commander in chief, for many of us, just aren't worth the rewards. However, the choice of moves is always ours to make.

We can easily see how the issue of choice affects a career similar to our own. As an example, say you're working in San Francisco. You own a small sailboat and divide your time between the water and the mountains. The kids are doing well in school, which is located around the corner. Both your parents and your spouse's parents live ten minutes away and are great baby-sitters. Life couldn't be better as a second-line manager in a growing company.

Monday morning, your manager calls you into her office and, with a big smile, offers you a promotion to branch manager of the Cheyenne, Wyoming, office. This is an important opportunity, as that office has been having some problems. Your boss trusts you to straighten things out. Clearly, this is one of those game challenges you should take.

However, when you go home with the good news, your family has other thoughts. They're not willing to move away from family, friends, and the ocean. No way! So the next morning, you thank your boss for the offer, but explain that now is just not the right time for you to accept the position. Maybe next year.

At that point, you've made a move on the game board. You had a choice, and you chose to go with the family team rather than the work team. Sure, the choice wasn't easy, but *choice* is what the game is all about. By the way, the opening is still available, and someone must fill it. You can be sure that four or five of your co-workers will gladly move to Cheyenne for a promotion. The move for them will be upward, while, at least for the short term, you will likely remain in San Francisco as a second-line manager.

For those who want to play hardball, for those who *really* want to reach that top rung of the ladder, no sacrifice is too great. That's what makes the game so fascinating. It's guided by rules, moves, and countermoves, and consists of a series of trade-offs we choose to make or not make.

If you're willing to play the game for upward mobility versus maintaining current status and are willing to dedicate extra hours to improve the strategy and execution of your game, the rewards are advancement within your chosen career. However, you must develop your own game plan and execute the plan in order to maximize wins and minimize losses. Along the way, you will find that you are in total control of your own destiny. It is completely your choice.

The purpose of this book is to introduce you to the major elements of the game. The charts are designed to help you assess yourself and your developmental requirements as you create a personal game plan.

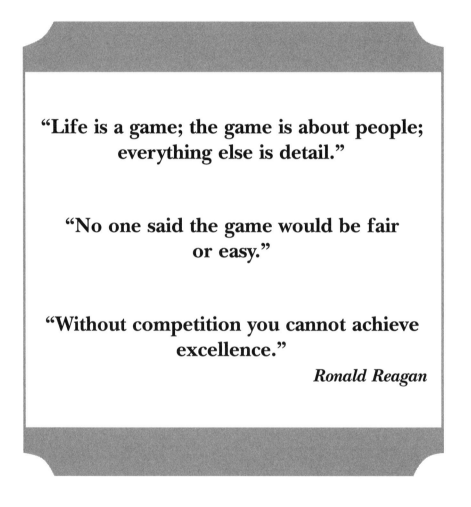

"Life is a game; the game is about people; everything else is detail."

"No one said the game would be fair or easy."

"Without competition you cannot achieve excellence."

Ronald Reagan

CHAPTER 2

Reading the Environment

Successful play in any organization requires careful attention to the work environment. We find that the best players are those who work hard to familiarize themselves with the rules of the organizational structure. They understand rules most of us have buried at the subconscious level, and they eagerly adapt to changing requirements.

The Japanese are a good example in this area. About four decades ago, they embarked on a farsighted mission to learn about the American business culture. They enrolled in our finest universities, and hired our best consultants. They studied, pondered, and absorbed our business sense. Then they began to manufacture shiploads of notoriously inferior consumer items. They had learned our game but were struggling desperately with quality.

For a full decade, at least, the "Made in Japan" label sold more extended warranties than any salesman! But somewhere along the way, sometime between the Korean War and the Vietnam War, they got the hang of it and have since built an international reputation as quality manufacturers.

The Japanese became experts in reading our business environment and converting it to their advantage. They looked at our game board, adopted our rules, and then, some years later, beat us soundly at our own game.

The Shared Environment

If we are to recapture the playing field at every level (individual, national, and international), we must redirect our efforts, as did the Japanese, and focus on learning to read the environment in which this game is played. Just like the opening in Cheyenne, Wyoming, there are plenty of other individuals and nations who will happily fill the position if we hesitate.

To understand the nature of a work environment, I have asked seminar participants over the last eighteen years to describe their organizations. In every type of organization, whether business, military, government, academia, or non-profit, many described their environment using the following words:

- Traditional
- Conservative
- Innovative
- Downsizing
- Team Oriented
- Empowerment
- Ownership
- Chain of Command
- Image Conscious
- Technically Oriented
- Political

- Service Oriented
- Results Oriented
- People Oriented
- Changing
- Quality Conscious
- Diversity Oriented
- Community Minded
- Line vs. Staff
- Merit Oriented
- Policy Bound
- Competitive

Rarely will my audience require adjectives other than these to describe their workplace. In fact, organizations share many similarities at this basic level, not only in our country, but all around the world as well. But then, they *must* share similarities to effectively communicate with other organizations. They all must speak the same business language, the origin of which can be traced back more than 700 years to the beginning of the British Empire. The global economy is now a reality since the fall of communism as we knew it; the world, in essence, is playing by the same set of rules.

Where Did It All Begin?

Every culture has a beginning. Once a custom or practice is repeated over and over again, it is eventually incorporated into the group's value system and becomes a standard or norm. These norms are not always written down but usually are passed to the next generation, either by role models or through stories. Eventually these standards and norms make up what I call cardinal rules, those rules that rarely, if ever, have exceptions.

To understand our current unwritten rules, one must apply one of those cardinal cules. The rule simply states, "Whoever is at the top of a pyramid has the right and the responsibility to make the rules." Subsequently, with the rise of the British Empire to the top of the world pyramid (it was once said that "The sun never sets on the British Empire"), they had the right to make the rules. It is no accident that every Russian, German, Japanese, and American child learns English in school. Why? Because England said the world would speak English, and it does. We will examine in a later chapter the other influences England has had on the game.

Culture Says It All

Every identifiable group has a culture. The Irish have theirs, as do Italians, Mexicans, Germans, and African-Americans. Within these groups there are a number of subcultures, such as women, the elderly, disabled, and young people. Whenever a group can be found whose members share a common set of beliefs, customs, values, language, and traditions that are passed from generation to generation, you have a culture. Business organizations, the military, and the government, to name a few, all have cultures. These organizational cultures are responsible for shaping every rule we must follow to be rewarded within these environments.

An appreciation of group culture is vital to individual advancement. If you were to invite a friend to a party, the friend, if very different from you (background, language, lifestyle, position, etc.) will be in an awkward environment as soon as he enters the room. He more than likely will not be comfortable; he probably wouldn't fit in; he might be different from the others in every regard, including dress, speech, and conversation. He is from a different culture, and will not be totally accepted until he adapts to the culture of the group attending the party. Another invitation might be slow in coming if he is too much out of step with the language, because people who disrupt the harmony of the group are often excluded.

The culture of the work environment is similar to the social one, and the ramifications are just as severe in a career as they are in a social setting. The implementation of the business culture is so rigid, in fact, that whenever a person violates one of its rules, the offender's career is jeopardized.

Languages and Their Impact on Advancement

When we speak of a person's organizational language, we are referring to much more than word usage. Organizational language is *total* communication, encompassing both the verbal and non-verbal behaviors. It includes verbal interplay, manner of dress, attitude, non-verbal cues, and the full gamut of communication skills, which, when combined, determine the impact of personal interaction and perceptions.

For example, everyone in business speaks some form of the business language. The language you display is directly related to success both inside and outside your corporation. Neither your manager nor your clients will trust you if they don't understand or respect the language you are speaking.

Although we will discuss at length the hierarchy of the organizational game, following is our game board divided into seven leagues, which represent positions within the organizational structure. Every job in the organization, whether business, military, or education, falls into one of these categories. Each league also has its own distinctive language.

As an individual moves up the career ladder, he discards or adds to his language from the previous league and adapts to the language of the new league. Failure to make these changes means he will stand out like the friend at the cocktail party. And as a result, will be rejected by peers and not seen as high potential by managers and executives.

There are many things that separate the different languages within groups. They involve such things as educational background, social activities, cultural interest, dress, and work

Socio-Economic Class Titles

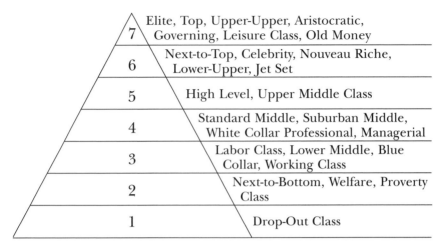

7	Elite, Top, Upper-Upper, Aristocratic, Governing, Leisure Class, Old Money
6	Next-to-Top, Celebrity, Nouveau Riche, Lower-Upper, Jet Set
5	High Level, Upper Middle Class
4	Standard Middle, Suburban Middle, White Collar Professional, Managerial
3	Labor Class, Lower Middle, Blue Collar, Working Class
2	Next-to-Bottom, Welfare, Proverty Class
1	Drop-Out Class

values. Each of them must be overcome if the next position is to be reached.

Fluency—The Automatic Answer

Here is an example of a man unaware of language and its importance to his career:

An executive in a large engineering firm needs to fill a vacancy. After reviewing fifteen files, he narrows his options to three candidates for the position. He wants to interview each of the finalists in person, as each has impressive credentials and a solid history of work performance.

It turns out that the first candidate never has a chance. He's an excellent worker—all right, a great worker. He's always on time, always has a positive disposition, and works hard. However, on the day of the interview, he offers a weak handshake, mumbles his replies, and avoids eye contact. He doesn't stand a chance. With three very qualified individuals available, being an excellent engineer is just one of the requirements. At this point what matters is that the candidate doesn't know the behavior expected of him and, therefore, is immediately eliminated.

The simple fact is, the executive must find some reason to eliminate two of the three final candidates outside of work performance. The lack of business fluency has provided ample reason for eliminating candidate number one. If the engineer had been fluent in the required culture, he would have been a stronger candidate. Fluency is the ability to communicate and fit into an environment without conscious thought.

Consider your ability to communicate in your native language. Words flow out automatically, below your conscious level. But should you attempt to learn a new language, say French, then you must certainly think about each word in order to present your ideas.

The more fluent a person is in any language or culture, the more comfortable he will make other people who are actively involved in the same language. And that comfort level among people translates into the crucial notion of *acceptance*. If we are *not* fluent, and must carefully choose every utterance, then the listener becomes uncomfortable. If we are uncomfortable with people, we won't be rude, but we won't invite them into our circle or spend much time around them. The rule of acceptance is true of every culture in the world, whether it's the business culture, the family culture (every family has a relative that just doesn't fit), or ethnic cultures. If a person is not accepted in ethnic or racial cultures, they will often be labeled as "sellouts" (an Oreo in the black culture or a banana in Asian cultures are labels often applied in these situations).

We must not forget that this is a people game. When a person attempts to move up in an organization but fails to display the cultural fluency required of that next level, he will normally be rejected by members of that group. Players do not advance very far up the ladder until they show signs of being able to play with ease, or fluency, on the upper steps. So there is an element of elimination built into the hierarchy that says, "In order to advance, you must be fluent in the next level's language." Another way of stating this is: "You must look and act the part before you will ever be considered for the part."

Exchanging Chips

We're in a game whose outcome will always be dictated by other people in our organization. In our day-to-day interactions with these people, we constantly exchange what I call the "chips" of life.

You can hand off a positive or a negative chip, a smile or a frown, a word of encouragement or discouragement. You can be a team player or a team distraction. The serious game player will understand the importance of these chips so as to bank as many positive ones as possible. For invariably, when upper management meets behind the closed door of the conference room, all the negative chips will surface. So we want to manage them, spread the good chips around, and keep the bad ones to ourselves.

P.I.E. — A Formula for Success

There are three elements important to players who want to fine tune their skills and move up in their profession. They must:

- *Perform* exceptionally well.
- Cultivate the proper *image.*
- Manage their *exposure* so the right people will know them.

These three basic elements of the business language, **Per**formance, **I**mage, and **E**xposure (**P.I.E.**), are woven into every job category, into every advancement opportunity, and into every management decision in which promotions are considered. The problem with these three criteria is that they are not always known to the player. By far, the easiest one to figure out are the requirements surrounding performance. This is the one that drives the bottom line, the profit margin, the very existence of the organization. It is so important that most organizations do not leave employees the option to guess what is expected of them. It is normally spelled out in organizational and departmental action plans as well as in individual performance plans. In fact, very few workers operate without a performance plan to guide them or to use as a reference during the course of the year. This, along with the policies and practices of the organization, becomes part of the written rules. More than likely, however, you do not have an annual image or exposure plan to guide you through the mine fields of the organization. These elements are such a strong part of the working culture that they reside at the subconscious level for most people. As a result, they often are neither written nor spoken.

Each of the three P.I.E. elements carries a different weight in upward mobility. All three are essential to promotion, but they have different roles and weights relative to their impact on long-term success. The breakdown is as follows:

- Performance = 10%
- Image = 30%
- Exposure = 60%

Shocking? It was for me! That is until I examined the rationale for the weightings.

The first thing to consider is that our system rewards performance. Organizations pay for performance but tend to promote based on potential. This statement is pretty much on target. In the many years of examining organizational written policies, I have never seen a policy that states, "We will promote based on performance." However, any organization that has a merit pay system clearly demonstrates that the higher the performance level, the more money a person will receive. It becomes my own false conclusion that if they pay me the most, I should also be promoted first. The danger of this assumption is that you cannot automatically conclude that the skills used in your present job are the same skills needed at the next level. How often have you observed that the best engineer, after being made a manager, becomes a fish out of water and fails miserably? A different job, a different set of skills.

Because performance is so important, we will spend time in the next chapter reviewing many of the considerations that should be made in this area. Your performance objectives should be very clear to you—written, discussed, and reviewed often. Image and exposure (ninety percent of the upward mobility formula) often gets lost in the efforts of our daily mission. These two elements could be the reason for your career frustration; it was for me. But it is an area any player can control, if all of the rules of the game were known.

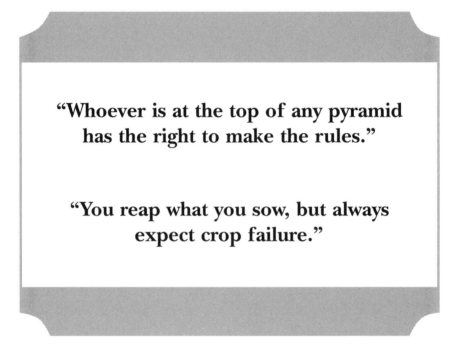

"Whoever is at the top of any pyramid has the right to make the rules."

"You reap what you sow, but always expect crop failure."

CHAPTER

3

Performance—
The Entry Ticket

From youth, we are taught that hard work is our ticket to the top. I still hear parents clucking about Bobby with his newspaper route or little Sue and her lemonade stand. They beam about values and the Puritan Work Ethic, and their eyes sparkle as they mention the possibility of their child in the White House.

If you just work hard enough, you can go anywhere. That's the message. To a degree, our parents and teachers are right. You can't get to the top unless you deliver first-class work to your manager, for the game of advancement is filled with excellent players. In order to even be considered for promotion, you must demonstrate both the willingness and the ability to perform in an outstanding manner. Those who cannot perform are not in the game.

So the first element of the P.I.E. formula begins with a slight irony. Although its weight accounts for only ten percent of the overall importance in a promotion, it's the ticket into the stadium. Without it, you won't even be admitted to the playing field.

You're Important, but . . .

If you look around your company, you can find others who could be considered your competition. This is no accident.

The replacement tables that most companies have adopted are designed to develop a pool of candidates who can fill any vacancy, which is sobering, for it means we can all be replaced within twenty-four hours!

In fact, *no one* is irreplaceable. We might look at certain executives and think of them as being necessary to the survival of the company, but I assure you that many of these so-called "critical players" have left companies, sometimes at the worst possible moment, and still the stock held its value, the business continued, and the payroll was met. In order to play the game as it must be played, we need to be aware of some basic realities. Understand that your performance must be top-notch, because you can be replaced, but also understand that there's a lot more to career advancement than doing an outstanding job.

It might be said that you are working *for* your organization to help it accomplish its mission (Performance), but you must work *on* yourself to be prepared for more responsibility via promotion (Image and Exposure).

Improve Your Performance

Before we get involved with improving your performance, you should be aware that your performance cannot be accomplished in a vacuum. You need a plan, one agreed to by both your manager and you. Your idea of success and your manager's may not be the same. This plan, once developed, forms the basis of your performance appraisal (an annual event in many organizations). Remember, as stated before, performance is the common denominator in the promotion process. If your performance is average or substandard, then your image and exposure, no matter how positive, will not secure you a promotion. Achieving an outstanding performance appraisal is vital if you are to progress.

So, to earn an outstanding performance appraisal, three elements are included: the plan, your performance, and the actual appraisal. Many people think that their involvement in this process begins and ends with their performance, and that it is up to their managers to appraise them. They believe if they perform well, a good appraisal will follow. It might, but it is by no means guaranteed. There are, however, some "game moves" that you can make that would increase the likelihood of your performance appraisal being outstanding.

The Performance Plan

Your organization may not have a formal appraisal system, but that should not be a reason to prevent you from initiating the process. Remember, the appraisal process is a way of communicating your contributions to your manager and should not be viewed as a tool of torture. Even when a formal appraisal system exists, managers are frequently reluctant to appraise their employees. The time it takes to outline specific objectives and the rating criteria, necessary for accurate appraisals, often falls well down on the priority list. Without these criteria being defined for each individual, it is all but impossible to appraise performance, and there is a tendency for managers, in an effort to be fair, to lump all of their employees in the satisfactory category. This, however, does little to distinguish you from your fellow employees. If your organization does not have a formal appraisal system, it is even more critical that you engage in a process similar to the one described in this chapter.

This kind of situation presents a real opportunity for you to make a couple of strategic moves on the game board. Instead of waiting for a performance plan that may never come, prepare your own. First, determine your manager's key measurements. Then link your duties to these measurements. Break your job duties down to accomplish three or four major tasks. Be specific as to what you have to do to earn an outstanding rating. Assign a percentage to each task, giving the heaviest weighting to those that are most important.

Your next step is to schedule an appointment with your manager. You want her to know how important receiving an outstanding performance rating is to you. Get an agreement as to what she feels constitutes an outstanding performance and what help you might need from her. Once this has been done, volunteer to submit the final plan with the changes. In submitting your final plan, specify the agreed upon time frame for your appraisal and reaffirm that you will periodically check with her to be certain that you are on track. It is up to you to ensure that your performance plan is a working document.

Over time, your performance plan may become obsolete. Your objectives can change dramatically with the adding of assignments or changes in their priority. If this occurs, you may choose to start the process again and have your manager close out your current plan with an appraisal, assuming enough time has elapsed. It is important for you and your manager, during your periodic meetings, to review the plan and make the necessary changes to keep it current. This will let your manager know that you regard this process as important. What do you accomplish by taking the lead role in the performance planning process?

- You ensure that you understand what your manager expects from you;
- You make certain that you both agree on what constitutes outstanding performance;
- You demonstrate to your manager that achievement of her goals is important to you;
- You use the process to achieve a superior appraisal, largely on your terms; and
- You help your manager, in that there is one less performance plan to write.

The Performance

Now that you have a working plan, what can you do to perform all tasks in an outstanding manner? All performance plans should contain provisions for accomplishing specific tasks in a given time frame, at a specified quality level and a minimum standard needed to meet these levels. However, the manner in which you exceed these standards is crucial to your success.

Job performance is made up of two major standards: objective and subjective. Both will be considered in your manager's evaluation of your performance. Let's look at them one at a time.

Objective Factors: These are the stated, written objectives of your assigned tasks. Did you produce the desired results, in the prescribed time frame, at the stated level of quality? It doesn't matter whether you are selling raincoats, producing widgets, creating reports, or performing research—did the final result meet or exceed your objective? If it didn't, you have cheated yourself and your organization. You might also assume that others who are more serious game players than you have performed their assigned tasks better.

Usually, many reasons can be given as to why your work effort and results may have fallen below expectations. There may have been interruptions; your manager may have assigned other tasks; you were helping a fellow worker; you were ill; you got involved with a different and/or more interesting project. Of course, these are all excuses, and are invalid. Unless your manager tells you differently, new assignments are in addition to your current responsibilities. Doing someone else's work, or performing other tasks that you feel will help the team is just fine, *if* you have already accomplished your assigned tasks in an outstanding manner. If you haven't, then you are putting your appraisal in jeopardy. If there are valid reasons for not performing your job, make certain that your manager is informed and agrees with them.

Subjective Factors: These are the unwritten rules closely associated with your task(s), and they are as important as the objective factors. Your performance of these tasks is crucial and usually determines the difference between an average and outstanding evaluation. The subjective factors are difficult to quantify because their evaluation depends on individual interpretation and assessment. Many of these unwritten elements have to do with the presentation of your final product. Let's assume the task involves written communication. Before you launch into the project, there are some additional game moves you can make that will increase your chance for success.

Shortly after your manager has assigned you the task, set aside some quiet time to ponder the project. After you have thought the project through and have a plan, create three documents: (1) a restatement of your understanding of the project and the results to be achieved; (2) a work plan with a schedule of completion dates for the various milestones associated with the project; and (3) an outline or description of how the end result will be presented. Review these documents with your manager, seeking her concurrence with your methods, time frames, and the approximate length and format of the final product. Ask for her advice and guidance. Having done this, you will be in a much better position to know the final product your manager is expecting.

During the development process, schedule brief progress meetings with your manager. People are different. If you have a "hands on" manager, don't resent her help—welcome it. If she is not, at least you are keeping her current on the status of your project. Pay close attention to the following aspects of the final document:

- Does it contain the required information?
- Does it read and flow well?
- Is it to go out under your signature or hers?
- Does it require a cover memo and/or an executive summary?
- Are the punctuation and spelling letter-perfect?
- Are all claims substantiated with supporting documentation?

- Is the distribution list complete and accurate?
- Is the document organized according to your approved outline?
- Are you prepared to answer questions about facts, conclusions, or recommendations that appear in the document?

A politician recently said, "The devil is in the detail." Be certain that the impact of your work isn't diminished by misspelled words, a name left off of the distribution list, unsubstantiated claims, or a careless oversight. It is not your manager's responsibility to correct your errors and oversights. With any project that you are responsible for, this is merely "completed staff work." But completed staff work can make any project succeed or fail.

Do not wait until the due date to submit your final product. Allow for time to make corrections, additions, and adjustments. Most likely, if you have been sufficiently thorough in keeping your manager informed, last minute changes won't be required. At this point you can only be guilty of submitting your finished product early!

The accomplishment of the objective and subjective tasks are of equal importance. Most people fail because of lack of close attention to the subjective portion of their tasks. Ask yourself some key questions about your finished product.

- Am I proud of this work?
- Would I have done it better if I were doing it for myself or for the president of the company?
- Have I done my best?

- How does this project rate with the performance plan criteria established with my manager?

If you are honest with yourself and your work can pass this type of scrutiny, then chances are you have done the job in an outstanding fashion and your manager will be thrilled with the result.

But, wait a minute. Didn't we state earlier that performance constitutes a relatively small percentage of those factors that determine promotability? Yes. Aren't image and exposure key? Yes.

Here is a question for you to ponder. Do you think a person could perform in an inferior manner and still have a "good image?" Suppose for a moment that the report you submitted was incomplete, sloppy, full of factual errors, and submitted late. Not only would your performance appraisal suffer, but there is no way your image would escape untarnished. You can go a long way toward building a good image by performing your work in an outstanding manner. Image messages in the performance of the task may provide important insights to your manger that you possess many of the qualities required of a good manager. Some of these positive messages might include:

- Uncomplaining
- Well Organized
- Productive
- Self Starter
- Thorough
- Creative Thinker

- Pays Attention to Detail
- Understands Our System
- Articulate
- Requires Little Supervision
- Reliable
- Ambitious

Not a bad list of ammunition to carry into any competitive job battle!

The Appraisal

The appraisal gets us back to the people game. Every appraisal will be delivered by a person, who as an individual has quirks, hot buttons, pet peeves, hopes, wishes, etc. This person will usually be your manager and is crucial to your career success. If you are not keeping her happy, then all of your efforts will be fruitless. This is so basic that it is always surprising when I discover that so many employees do not get along with their manager. If you happen to fall into this category, it is up to you to fix the problem. Do not wait for your manager to address the matter. It is not your manager's job to get you to like her. Respond to your manager as if she were the company president. Your mindset should be that you are one of her key employees, contributing to the accomplishment of her goals. It is your job to make her look good all of the time. The best way to do this is to complete your assigned tasks in a superior manner. Once this is done, if time permits, volunteer for additional duties.

The message here is that while performance only counts ten percent when evaluating promotional candidates, your performance is a major contributor to your image. Performance shows that you bring worth to the organization. So make no mistake, performance is a critical ingredient in the overall success formula. Outstanding performance is the admission ticket into the stadium where the game will be played.

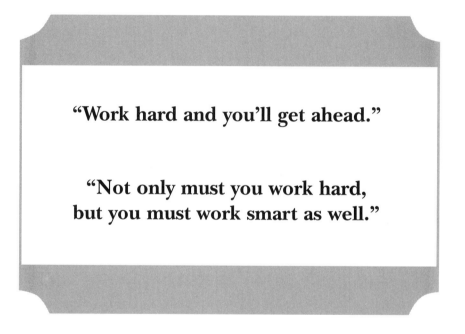

"Work hard and you'll get ahead."

"Not only must you work hard,
but you must work smart as well."

CHAPTER 4

Image

From the moment you step out of your car and cross the parking lot each morning, you're a visible expression of where you are in the business culture, and where you expect to go.

Image is an important tie-breaker when senior management reaches into the pool of excellent performers to promote the next candidate. A good image accounts for thirty percent of the weight given to a promotion. That is triple the attention afforded performance. Above all else, we must keep in mind the powerful impact visual communication plays in this people game.

Image includes many areas of personal expression, the way you walk, the way you sit, the clothes you wear, your pleasant (or foul) demeanor. Everything about a person, from dress to speech to attitude, sends a strong message to business associates. Image says "I'm ready" or "I'm not ready" to play the game seriously at the next level.

Periodically, we should take a moment to review the signals we are sending. Our foremost question is, "What messages am I sending, and are they the messages that will move me in the direction I have chosen?" If we don't occasionally spend some time in this candid assessment, then we're probably not playing the game very well.

The Non-Verbal Message . . .
Sight Over Sound

Your non-verbal messages are a large part of the image you project. When we divide our communications into three areas—non-verbal, verbal, and tone—the non-verbal message is by far the most important. Martin Luther King's words "I Have a Dream" were impressive when heard; however, if you saw him deliver the speech and felt the passion and animation of his delivery, he truly inspired a nation to change.

Just as the three P.I.E. elements are weighted by importance, so are the three communication channels. They are non-verbal, verbal, and tone of voice. About seventy percent of the information we give credence to after a conversation or meeting comes from non-verbal messages, such as eye movement, smiles, and posture of the people we see. Tone of voice accounts for only about ten percent. The words we hear represent about twenty percent of the messages we trust.

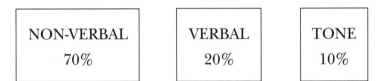

NON-VERBAL	VERBAL	TONE
70%	20%	10%

Most of us understand the importance of the non-verbal message, and we pass our experience along to others. "Cut your hair," we advise teenagers on the way to their first interview. "Shine your shoes. You'll never get a job looking like that!" Our focus is on image because we know, intuitively, that interviewers form their opinion largely based on first impressions. Who has not heard the expressions, "First impressions are lasting impressions," or "You don't have a second chance to make a good first impression."

Interviewers normally take about twenty seconds to form an opinion of a job applicant, while the next thirty minutes might well be spent collecting information to verify that opinion.

Managers typically make the same quick judgement of you and your co-workers. They have to. They meet many people throughout the day, and to keep from becoming bogged in the details, they quickly evaluate and then move on to other tasks.

Our non-verbal vocabulary is important because it is our original language, coming even before speech. Anyone who has communicated with a baby knows that each person understands the other. The parent's side will sound like this:

"Jason! Take that out of you mouth, son."

"Come on, now. Take it out."

"Jason, don't look at me that way. I said, 'Take it out!'"

Of course, Jason hasn't said an intelligible word, but both he and his parent have communicated, one with words, and the other with expressions and actions.

Throughout our life, we have heard the old platitudes, "Seeing is believing," "A picture is worth a thousand words," and "Talk is cheap." As parents and as managers, we begin to understand that it is impossible to motivate any individual, or even to create the environment for motivation, if we do not set the example through our own actions, "Leading by example" or "becoming a role model" are not empty expressions.

When parents walk into their children's room with a cigarette in one hand and a drink in the other, proclaiming "There will be no smoking or drinking from you guys," or when a manager says, "I want everyone at their desks and ready to work at 8:30 a.m. sharp," but then he consistently shows up around 9:00 a.m., then the parent's and the manager's perturbed complaint, "Don't they understand English?" loses much of its punch. Employees do, indeed, hear your voice, but they obey the non-verbal message. The best way to be a truly successful leader is by example: Actions must support the words spoken. This conclusion conforms to our reliance on the non-verbal language we have used since birth.

We can cry, "Don't do as I do, do as I say," and we think that releases us from the responsibility of leadership by example. But remember, seventy percent of everything we absorb is non-verbal in nature. So, even though you might want to pass on your philosophy, you cannot teach with words. You must "Walk the talk" and "Practice what you preach" because as we all know "Talk is cheap."

Dress

Your business wardrobe is very, very important to your career. Serious players dress at least one level above their present position on the pyramid. Dress is a badge in business that states emphatically: "I want you to consider my fluency at this level." Dressing in that special business outfit at interview time is saying, "I fit here, and I'm serious about business; hire me."

Because your clothing will have a greater impact on more people than anything else you normally do in your work day, your most important business decision may be made before you leave the house; that decision will be made at your wardrobe closet.

Like most of my lessons, I learned this one the hard way early in my career with IBM. I was new to the marketing department, working, studying, and exploring this new environment. I had been on the job just long enough to begin to feel comfortable. And I was fitting in. I was going to make it.

That thought was heightened one morning as my boss delayed an important meeting to speak to me outside his office. His natural forthrightness seemed accepting of my newness, although this morning his eyes were twinkling with amusement.

"Harvey," he chuckled, "I see you have a part-time job." A nice smile broadened across his face, and without offering a clue to the meaning of that statement, he hurried off to his meeting.

"What do you mean, a part-time job?" I yelled after him.

"Well, you're driving a bus this evening, aren't you?" he shot back. "You've got your bus driver shirt on again." Secretaries and my co-workers around the office pretended that they hadn't heard his comment.

My "bus driver" shirt! He was referring to the blue shirt I was wearing. It was my carefully considered rejection of the cloud of white all about me. As the only black person in the department, I already looked different from my peers. So I really didn't see why I should conform to the unwritten white shirt code. I was going to stand out regardless of my dress.

A week later, this same manager met with me, this time in his office with the door shut. And this time, he wasn't smiling. He stepped around his desk and grabbed me lightly around my neck concealing my tie.

"Harvey," he said evenly. "What color tie do you have on?" His hand kept me from looking down, but after a moment of hesitation, I remembered.

"My blue striped tie."

"Right. Now Harvey, what color shirt do you have on?"

I had him on this one as well. "My blue shirt," I replied.

"That's correct." Then he continued. "Tell me, how many times have you looked down at your shirt today?"

"Three or four times, I guess." I felt like a new Army recruit, firing away at the drill sergeant's questions. "OK, Harvey," he said. "Now, what does the color blue feel like?" His hand remained at my throat.

"What do you mean?" I responded, searching for the right answer. "You can't *feel* the color blue."

"Then let me summarize," he whipped. "You have only seen your shirt three times today, while I have been looking at it for three hours. Furthermore, the color blue has no feeling at all for you, but I can tell you exactly how it makes me feel every time I look at it. It makes me feel like you don't want to be a part of our team!

"Now, if you don't see your shirt as often as I do, and if you don't feel as deeply about the color blue as I do, then why do you insist on dressing for yourself and not for me?" He saw by my facial expression that he had made a good point.

Most of us tend to save our best suits for carefully selected events. If we have an important meeting, if the president is in town for a visit, or if we're trying to close a big sale, we reach for our best.

But consider what you're saying when you do that. If you only wear your best clothes for a special occasion that might happen once a week, then in ten days, you're assuming you will only be seen by an influential person twenty percent of the time. This means that the other eighty percent of the time you will have to be very lucky not to meet someone who will form an unfavorable opinion of you, based solely on your dress. Do you want to gamble at those odds?

Serious game players eliminate luck. They wear their "best suit" every day of the week, always prepared for that surprise visit from the president. But that means paying some dues. For one thing, in large organizations this usually means you might as well get comfortable, because you will normally wear that uniform every day.

The language of serious players at or near the top of their organization is one of conservative and traditional dress. Consequently, if employees come to work in high fashion, true business people will dismiss them as unqualified pretenders in the game. The unspoken, even subconscious, thought is: "You don't want to be here. You don't agree with the organization's value system, and being on this team is not a priority. And, if all of this is true, how can I possibly give you additional responsibility?" That's when careers stagnate, and often the employee doesn't realize that the reason can be traced back directly to dress.

But our work location has a casual dress policy—doesn't that exempt me from those rigid rules? Maybe. First, understand that casual dress is just another uniform. It does not mean that image will not be a factor in other people's perception of you. There is a gap between business casual and comfortable, even sloppy dress. It is important to notice that business casual dress at entry level versus business casual dress for executives is different. And so there are still dress "choices" to be made even in a casual dress environment.

Off with the Facial Hair

Early in my career, I had a mustache. Fortunately, I also had a manager who wasn't reluctant to coach his people, even in the more delicate "personal appearance" area. He approached me one day with a strange question.

"Do you think that your power and ability to do things are dependent upon your facial hair?" he asked. "Of course not," I laughed, knowing my mustache did not carry with it the powers of Sampson. "Well, then let me suggest something," he responded. "Try cutting it off and see how things work out. If they don't, you can always grow it back."

He was right. There was not much to lose by shaving the mustache off, but there could be a lot to gain. If you take a look at participants in a conservative business environment: (1) facial hair, both mustaches and beards, will be acceptable in some businesses in the professional ranks; (2) occasionally it will be found in middle management; (3) you will seldom find it at the senior manager; and (4) you will hardly ever find facial hair at the executive level.

Facial hair could be (depending on the organization) another trade-off, another choice, that you must consider if you elect to compete for a top position. For some people, shaving their mustache (as well as shaving their beard) will separate them from their peer group, even to the point of risking personal relationships. But the choice is definitely yours, and yours alone, to make. It is another reason why some people begin to fall away from rising in the pyramid. We can't have it all. Sometimes we must leave our peer group members behind in order to be president of the company, and sometimes it gets lonely. But the very shape of the game board indicates that we can't have a gang of people sitting at the top. Trade-offs eliminate everyone but the most serious players.

Be on My Team

Managers are remarkably tolerant of individuals who fail to produce at a level consistent with their capabilities, *as long as* their attitudes are positive and their willingness to improve is obvious. Even though these people will never advance very far, their jobs are seldom in jeopardy.

But woe be to the employee whose constant complaints sour an entire office. These people, even though their bottom-line results might be better than anyone else's in the company, are on the way out. They will be fired, at worst, and ignored, at best. Management can always find someone who can do the job and not destroy the team in the process.

Many of these disgruntled workers are riding the crest of individualism, where "doing your own thing" is their ultimate objective. I am often challenged that highlighting a set of rules or emphasizing certain standards of behavior that will be rewarded suggests conformity. "Conformity" is such a negative word for most of us. "Conformity" is that thing that strips us of our individuality and our cultures. However, the reality is that the organizational culture requires no more from us than any other culture. Did we not have to adapt or conform to the rules of our parent's home? Did we not adjust behaviors or conform to every teacher's classroom requirements? Does not every ethnic or racial group have standards they expect their members to uphold? Of course they do. It is safe to say that even non-conformist groups (e.g., punk rockers, cyclist groups, hippies) all require conformity to their rules if a person is to be accepted. To think that the work culture will not have standards for rewarded behavior is not realistic. Without standards, communication and trust would completely disappear. Teamwork and business relations would be non-existent. Anarchy would prevail.

We have seen the impact on children who come from homes that have not established and/or communicated values. Frequently, they appear out-of-control. There will be the same effect on employees who work in an organization that denies there are rules. Today, more than ever, there is a need to establish common values and objectives for the working unit. Will everyone in the organization choose to adapt to the executive values in a organization? Of course not. However, when the rules are known by all, all will have the freedom to choose.

How Can I Keep My Culture?

This is one of the toughest emotional battles anyone must take on if they have strong, well-defined cultural roots. Being forced to abandon cultural traditions to play the organization's game often feels like you are "selling out" and/or becoming someone you are not. This is a great concern for organizational America. With the talent pool at level two, three, and four becoming more racially and culturally diverse, organizations are realizing that to attract this new talent, the organizations culture must become more inclusive. These are the levels where cultural practices are still an integral part of an employee's life. In level three, to go back to "Little Italy" or the Polish, Irish, or black communities every night we know will often cause conflict of values, clashes of culture, and create moments of stress. If these conflicts or stressful situations become too extreme or happen too often, talented people will leave the work environment, particularly in occupations where there is a talent shortage. That individual can easily get a job in a more friendly and inclusive environment. At this level, many progressive organizations are creating through their diversity initiatives a more welcoming environment for people's differences. However, there are some harsh realities that apply to these situations. First, for a team player to allow cultural behaviors to dominate in a work team environment usually tells the organization that promotion to management for that individual is not practical. The logic is clear: If one chooses to practice only their cultural language and values, it would be extremely difficult for that person to be as effective communicating with and managing mainstream-oriented peers and employees with mainstream values. Other candidates that have adapted to the mainstream business culture are usually viewed as better qualified candidates.

The system becomes less accepting of cultural elements such as dress, language, traditions, and customs the higher you move up on the game board. At levels six and seven, rarely do you see a display of specific ethnic traits. Cultural values do, however, play an important role in every decision made by top executives. As examples of this, John F. Kennedy made decisions based on his upbringing in the Irish Catholic community, and Colin Powell makes decisions based on his cultural heritage both within and outside the United States. This occurs, of course, because of their past experiences and backgrounds, which allow all decisions to be filtered through those cultural lenses. At the same time, their decisions are heard and acted upon because they are delivered in the mainstream executive language.

When looking at culture, it is important to distinguish "values" and "fads." The lifespan of a "fad" is short, lasting several weeks, months, or a couple of years. Some examples of recent fads include: the baggy pants look, the decorative braids worn by many young African-American men, even wearing hairstyles with initials as part of the overall design. It is doubtful that many African-American men over the age of fifty would actively participate in these fads. However, the fads of the 1950s, 60s, and 70s would surely have involved many who were teenagers and young adults at that time, but all of these fads have long since faded away. Values, on the other hand, last much longer. Some may not change during a lifetime. Others may change based on personal experience or tragic circumstances.

The American business culture encourages the inclusion of fundamental ethnic and racial values such as "respect, hardwork, pride, and the equitable treatment of others." Hopefully, learning the executive language will never require the rejection of these important cultural concepts.

The current challenge for the organizational culture in our diverse society is to create environments that respect differences among people and allow those who do not choose the manager and/or executive value system to be comfortable being themselves. This can be done as long as the team remains productive.

In the competitive global environment of today, it makes sense that teamwork is becoming increasingly important. A hundred people going in a hundred different directions cannot take a team successfully to a desired objective. We must cooperate if we're going to truly be successful as a society, and more than ever before, we must display teamwork if our careers are going to continue to grow. Upper management is looking for team players to add to their candidate lists, because they haven't overlooked the success companies in other nations have enjoyed when they all pulled for a common goal.

The Japanese are excellent examples of how broad this willingness to adapt to team play has become. As I've mentioned, the Japanese, even with 6,000 years of tradition and history, have become very serious game players. They speak English. They will shake hands rather than bow. For sport, they will more than likely host you to a round of golf instead of attending a sumo wrestling match. These people are serious players, willing to adapt to the well-defined game rules. They have made choices.

The Japanese are also striking examples of the importance of dress in bridging cultural mistrust. We are also well aware that more than likely, we won't even be considered for a promotion unless we select the right dress. Still, we must be careful about placing the success of our careers solely on clothing. The game is so serious and so finely tuned at the top that those players can determine immediately whether you're dressed appropriately. However, they also recognize that just because we wear the right suit of clothes or the appropriate uniform, we still might not be fluent at that level.

That's where many of us get caught. We are willing to play the game to a limit, but not all the way. If we fail to play all-out, we are setting ourselves up for certain defeat. Anytime a competitive game is played and there are several people who will do anything to win, while we are only halfway into it, we might as well save ourselves the trouble because we have lost from the very beginning. A true player will want to beat those individuals who are acting and doing their very best. When the game is won on those high standards, it is truly a victory. I don't want to be rewarded in a game that demands one hundred percent by giving only fifty percent, because then it is a shallow victory. The major plus to the competitive nature of the game is obvious when all players are playing by the same rules. President Reagan, in his 199th State of the Union speech, stated, "Without competition you cannot have excellence." With the rules known to all, the organization and our society are the big winners by simply raising the standard of excellence.

In addition to dress, attitude is crucial in presenting a good image. No manager wants someone who says, "That's not my job." Think of a sports team, where everyone benefits when the team wins. It would be absolutely ridiculous if a quarterback should fumble the ball, and as it spins to a slow stop, a lineman walks past it with a shrug, saying "I'm not going to pick it up. That's not my job."

Yet, how many times do we see that happening in our work environment? How often do we see people concentrate solely on their own situation and let the team fend for itself, without support and/or encouragement? As players, and we are all on teams of one kind or another, we must not only be able and willing to take risks for the team, but also give up some of our individuality for the good of the team, as well.

Never go to a supervisor with a problem for which you have not considered a solution. As a good team player, you ought to be astute enough to offer suggestions. You should constantly reappraise your environment by asking, "If my group encounters problems, what am I going to do about it?"

We are all on some kind of team in our jobs and are frequently involved in team activities, which often require a specific team uniform. Teams and dress share important roles in business. Dress becomes a common bond or bridge that makes everyone equal—women, minorities, young—it doesn't matter. If you care enough to prove your enthusiasm for the game, anyone will be accepted. Once again, this is a people game, and people will invite others into their group when they feel comfortable, no matter who they are.

The Team Player Attitude

Your attitude toward your team members, your management and your company is crucial to your success, and to the team as a whole. Some of the more important aspects of a positive attitude are:

- A willingness and desire to actively participate on the team.
- A willingness to take calculated and well-planned risks for the sake of the team's success (individual success will surely follow).
- The demonstration of flexibility, understanding, and acceptance of the fact that a team may have to change direction many times. In a competitive environment, the team looks for individuals who do not drag their feet, who do not talk about the "good old days" and the way

the job "used to be done," and who are willing to take on new directions and adapt quickly to change.

- The ability to demonstrate a willingness to solve problems. Managers quickly identify those people who are constant complainers but who do very little to correct the situation. A team player offers solutions. One of the cardinal rules of the game is to "**never bring anyone a problem without a solution**." This applies, of course, to an employee bringing a problem to his or her manager, but it also applies to a boss giving feedback to an employee, a parent to a child, a friend to a friend, etc. If you have thought enough to recognize that a problem exists, you have the responsibility to also think of a possible solution. This is the difference between complainers, a discontent; a grumpy person versus a team player, a problem-solver, an ally, and a person who wants to help.

- The willingness to help in all situations. The old "It's not my job" sentiment cannot be tolerated by teams that are in highly competitive environments. Successful teams are looking for people who do not narrowly interpret job descriptions. It is expected that anything that goes wrong will be resolved by anyone on the team who sees the problem.

- To show a desire for the team to win. This is difficult for us to do simply because we have just come out of a number of years where the individual was most important—the "Me" generation, which championed the "I want, I think, I have, I ought to do, I have a right" philosophy. Full commitment to team success is critical.

- There are any number of additional qualities that indicate that one has a positive attitude. In addition to those already stated, supporting your manager, being well liked by your peers, going the extra mile to get a job done right, requiring little or no management time in the accomplishment of your tasks, and being a self-starter are all evidence of an employee with a "good attitude."

Now, because of fierce domestic and international competition, we are discovering that we cannot afford to be a nation of individuals. We are starting to talk about teamwork and are trying, in many organizations, to give rewards to those individuals who show a team effort. This is clearly the trend for the next several decades, at least.

Unfortunately, the events of September 11, 2001, has brought all Americans and most of the free world to a realization that we are truly together in basic issues of living a free existence in unity. Common effort will be the key factor for us to prevail in our basic way of life. It is in times like these that individual differences just don't seem that important.

Friends Implore . . . Quit Playing!

One of the most difficult parts of playing all-out is the realization that you must sometimes leave friends behind. When you know your goal is to participate to the fullest, you will find people talking about you. They'll ask you not to play the game, saying things like, "John, what are you doing dressed like that? You look like you're going to church. Come on, loosen up.

We're more casual than that. You don't have to wear that tie." Or the message might be "Why are you going back to school? You don't need any more education around here."

Your friend is really saying, "John, I know you're sending messages to the people above, and I know that eventually they will see you and move you up. We want you to stay here with us." They honestly like you. They don't want to let you go. You ought to be prepared for friends and co-workers to make you uncomfortable when you begin to change and speak the business language of a higher level.

It's like the high school friends we all left behind. We swore allegiance and friendship all our life, but when we went away to college and returned for the summers, we knew that we spoke different languages, and our lives would never be the same. This kind of "letting go" hurts so much that often this is the point where people say, "That's too high a price for me to pay to play the game. I do not want to let this set of friends go." And that constitutes a move on the game board—another trade-off has been made! As we move closer to the top, the decisions and choices become more difficult. However, they are still our choices. We are one hundred percent in control of ourselves in this game.

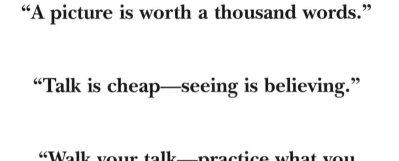

"A picture is worth a thousand words."

"Talk is cheap—seeing is believing."

"Walk your talk—practice what you preach."

"You might not get a second chance to make a good first impression."

CHAPTER 5

Exposure

The Game Begins

Exposure is the element of the P.I.E. formula that has the greatest impact on your career. This is the area of the game where all of our choices are played out and experienced. These experiences allow us to evaluate whether we are content at our current level or to determine the choices we must make to change our current level, up or down. Most of all, exposure introduces one of the most powerful facts in the game of life: that **you can't do it alone!** The "it" in this case is everything outside of our internal thought processes. It covers all of the areas and events where we must have help. Think about the raise you want. Can you give it to yourself? Of course not. How about the promotion you seek? Can you make that decision on your own? Sometimes we wish we could, but the reality is this: We always need other people to help accomplish any goal we want to obtain. Still not convinced? Have you ever made a sale without a person having to decide if they want to buy from you? Or joined a group or club without someone in the group extending an invitation? More than likely, the answer to both of the questions is a resounding NO. It is exposure that brings us face to face with the fact that this is a people game. Our ability to become visible in a positive way and influence others who can help us reach our goals is one of the keys to this game.

The report card on your ability to perform in the exposure arena usually is determined in personal or family critical situations. For example, if you have just lost your job, do you have to fill out ten applications for employment and mail them to strangers who know nothing about you or can you call up two friends of yours with hiring authority and get employment without going through all of the administrative red tape normally connected with hiring? Can you get your son and daughter a little help when they apply to the U.S. Army Military Academy at West Point? Do they fill out one of the approximately 30,000 applications per year and hope for the best or can you call up your congressman (who you helped in their winning a congressional campaign) or General Jones (who serves with you on a local Chamber of Commerce Committee) and ask for their help? If either or both respond "I'll be happy to run some interference for your child," you have just capitalized on your exposure.

How to Get Exposure Inside the Organization

It is extremely important to gain, maintain, and enhance personal visibility and exposure. Prince Charles was born to be the King of England, just as the CEO's son or daughter has a ticket to the top. They have been taught to fill those positions from the day they were born, so as to ensure their fluency in their future top positions.

But there's hope for those of us born to the lesser ranks of life to reach the top—if that is your choice. In order for this to be done, however, we need to become fluent in upper level languages. We must work on gaining the exposure necessary to attract a sponsor to help us advance through the ranks. Here are some suggestions for gaining exposure and greater visibility within any organization. This list is not all inclusive. As you read it, make notes on other things you are currently doing for your career.

- *Volunteer for Internal Projects*
  This involves risk, which is often a deterrent. However, even if the project is not completely successful, the message of willingness and initiative will be conveyed.

- *Assume More Responsibility within a Specific Job Function*
  In the short term, this suggestion may not provide any additional compensation. The choice is whether to make short-term tradeoffs for potential long-term gains.

- *Get Involved in the Community*
  Most organizations maintain this area as a priority. In all cases, it demands extra time from anyone who participates. However, the return on this investment is twofold. First, the individual will have an opportunity to meet and work with representatives of other organizations, thereby increasing personal networks, and secondly, the organization receives public recognition through the efforts of the individual. In turn, the individual is placed in a positive light within the organization. Most importantly, the real benefit is that the community will enjoy the fruits of your labor.

- *Become Active in Board Service*
  This is one of the most important, yet the most overlooked, ways to gain exposure. Board service should be

a career objective. Service on boards allows the opportunity to utilize, fine tune, and polish existing skills, as well as develop new ones with minimal risks. Board service generally begins in the non-profit sector and through planning, demonstrated performance, and exposure can lead to positions on profit-making boards with compensation. Again, the benefit of this type of service is not only to the individual, but also to your organization and the organization you serve.

- *Participate in Company-Sponsored Activities*
  Occasionally, organizations will sponsor activities that present opportunities to interact with many levels of management. The perception is often that one must show up at the beginning and leave when the activity is officially over; however, this is not true in all cases. It is necessary for others to recall that an individual showed up, not necessarily that he or she stayed until the end. It is critical that company-sponsored events are viewed as quasi-social. These events are not set up for employees to necessarily "have a good time." Rather, they are designed to achieve a specific objective. Frequently, one of the major objectives is to establish a comfort level between executive team members and other employees. This may involve both the individual and family members. Naturally, if the event is also enjoyed, then all the better. Examples of company-sponsored activities include: holiday parties, picnics, cocktail parties, drinks after work, sports activities, and dinner parties.

- *Keep Abreast of Current State of the Art Techniques*
  Read and participate in discussions, meetings, and professional associations. Make it a point to be well versed in areas concerning the organization, as well as current events. A major complaint is that "Business is discussed all the time inside and outside the company." This is as it should be—people who are very serious about business talk about it constantly. Many times, at company-sponsored functions, business topics arise and your participation is expected and appreciated.

- *Visibly Demonstrate a Team Player Attitude*
  This includes adherence to dress codes, behavior dictates, peer associations, execution of skills, display of initiative, and loyalty to the company.

- *Be Willing to Learn New Skills and Experience Different Situations*
  In some cases, these activities will highlight areas needing further development. Don't be afraid to learn. People who are successful continually grow.

The suggestions listed above are not easy and are by no means the only ways to gain exposure. In order for any skill to be useful, each individual must determine career and lifestyle objectives and then decide whether the process for achieving them is worth the effort. Remember, before you reach the top, a great deal of effort will be required.

Business is a game, with a set of rules. Moves are made by each person within the parameters of those rules. The choice of moves has always, *and will always,* be up to the individual player.

How to Get Exposure Outside the Organization

For further clarification of exposure outside of the organization, it is necessary to look at the socio-economic levels that define lifestyles in our society. A major portion of the game is played among these levels, as this is where people more closely interact. The study of these various levels is a science known as sociology. As Americans, we want to believe that there is no class structure in our country; however, the idea of a classless society is a myth. It is natural for people to bond together in groups in which they are most comfortable. Class groups are formed by individuals who share similar characteristics, such as occupation, education, financial status, and common interests.

If you still have doubts whether classes exist, ask yourself, "How similar is your day, week, or month compared to a member of the Rockefeller family?" Unless you are in a group of people that represent less than five percent of the American population, then your lifestyle will probably be significantly different from the Rockefellers! I am not saying that a Rockefeller's lifestyle is better—it is just different.

The limitation with sociology is that it identifies the different levels in our society, but it does not explain how the system works. How do we move from one point on the game board to the next? What differences exist between the various levels? Who or what controls the movement of people? The answers to these questions are important to understanding and effectively playing "the game."

The Game Board Defined

In Chapter Two, we introduced the playing field through a pyramid model that corresponds to the socio-economic classes identified in the United States. These levels also correspond to levels within business, government, education, and the military. The business pyramid is shown in the diagram below.

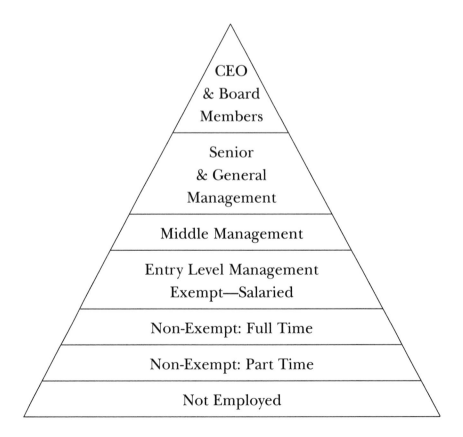

CEO & Board Members

Senior & General Management

Middle Management

Entry Level Management Exempt—Salaried

Non-Exempt: Full Time

Non-Exempt: Part Time

Not Employed

In order to understand the dynamics of the system, however, it is necessary to first understand a few critical rules.

"WHOEVER IS AT THE TOP OF A PYRAMID HAS THE RIGHT (AND OBLIGATION) TO MAKE THE RULES."

This rule applies to all existing pyramids: work, family, and social. Here is an example of how this rule applies in the family pyramid to which we might all be able to relate. Remember when you were fourteen years old and were supposed to be home by eight o'clock? However, on one occasion it was ten o'clock before you knew it and as you walked up the front steps, you knew you were in trouble. Before you abandoned all hope of survival, you may have tried this technique. You simply told your father or mother that you were old enough to know what to do, when to do it, how to take care of yourself, and would decide for yourself from now on what time you should come home! Well, this technique did not work in my house either! Whenever I attempted this strategy, my father's response was, "When you get a job and help pay some of these bills, maybe you can have some input around here. However, until that time, *as long as you live under this roof . . .!*" Dad was reminding me of the rules that exist in families as well as work. *People at the top of the pyramid structure make the rules!* This rule becomes helpful when any player is confused about an action or direction they should take in their environment. If this should happen, we need to look to the actions of people at the top and we will be able to observe the rewarded behaviors.

The responsibility of anyone who is at the top of the pyramid is heavy. If you want to communicate one code of conduct you expect in the organization, you must be willing to model the desired behaviors. You must "walk your talk" and "lead by example" if you want others to follow or support your rules. This applies not only to running the entire organization but also to managing any specific department. "Practice what you preach," is the guiding philosophy.

In Chapter Two we also introduced the concept of the game board. It might be helpful here to define the board in greater detail and uncover the dynamics of how the system works.

England's Influence

Although Americans come from all over the world, England's influence on us and the rest of the world cannot be denied.

England has given the world many things. For example, if you wanted to socialize with the people at the very top of any society in the world you would consider learning one or all four of the following social activities: golf: started in Scotland over 500 years ago (St. Andrew's); tennis: over 250 years ago (Wimbleton); sailing; and yachting. England, being an island, utilized the water, both militarily and socially. In addition, the top of the social structure always rallied around activities surrounding horses such as polo, fox hunting, and horse racing, often called "the sport of kings." In the United States we often call this group "the horsy set."

It is interesting to note that both China and Russia built their first golf courses about ten years ago. Since they have joined the global economy, it is necessary for them to make visiting worldwide top executives, politicians, and other power brokers comfortable. Vietnam, who most recently entered the game, has recently opened six golf courses. The Japanese, now veteran players of the game, cannot get enough of golf, even sponsoring a professional tour. In summary, you will never find an executive retreat anywhere in the world that will not be located near a body of water and will not have tennis courts or a golf course. Rarely will you find a bowling alley at these locations.

England also gave us our justice system of a trial by a jury of peers, representative democracy as a form of government, and the government structure of two houses of the legislature based on the House of Commons and the House of Lords. However, one of the most significant legacies the British Empire has passed down is its socio-economic class structure. The foundation of this structure and the various levels within it are built around the value system instilled in us by our parents, schools, and neighborhoods. Remember, in part, culture is a set of values passed from generation to generation. Everyone enters the game at the level of his or her parents at the time of his or her birth. Therefore, *we are all born into a class,* and as a result pick up the values of our parents and the general community in which we are raised.

It All Begins When . . .

It began for all of us the moment we were introduced to our parents, their values, and their lifestyles. Most of our values were formed at a very early age. According to Dr. Morris

Massey, a world-renowned expert on how our values are formed, he believes that "fifty percent of our values are locked in by the time we are five years old." I agree. If you want to check his premise—walk up to a five-year-old boy today and ask "Would you like to play with a doll?" Even in this age of enlightenment, most likely his response would be, "No, boys don't play with dolls!" A girl, when offered a gun or a truck will probably tell you that "Girls don't play with guns and trucks." As a society, we still bombard our children with stereotypical messages regarding interests and activities. For example, have you ever seen a boy featured in a Barbie doll ad? Is it any wonder that little boys are not comfortable playing with dolls?

By the time we reach ten years old, Dr. Massey says "that ninety percent of our values are formed. By this age we know what is good or bad, right or wrong." We record these messages in our gut level tape recorders to be played back when we need them later in life. By the time we reach twenty-one, our values are locked in for life. He suggests, however, with a "Significant Emotional Event" (S.E.E.), it can free us from past values and allow us to substitute new ones. In other words, something must really shake us up if we are to break away quickly from any of our instilled values. Personal experience allows us to shift our values more quickly.

For example, you might imagine someone taking a very closed-minded stand on the gay and lesbian issue. Statements like, "I think it's a mortal sin," "People like that are ruining our society," and "I'll never let one of those people in my house" would not be unusual comments coming from that individual. Let that same individual, who is a loving parent, get a call from their twenty-four-year-old son or daughter announcing that they are gay or lesbian; the entire core value of this individual will be challenged. If he keeps his values intact he or she will break contact with his child, never allowing them to come back home. The other option, and likely the one he might choose, is to go into his tape recorder and alter his opinion about gays and lesbians. In essence, change his values. To do so, however, usually takes a Significant Emotional Event.

To better understand the significance of this process, it is important to understand the role values play at each level. To know this is to understand the conflicts we have in deciding whether we want a lifestyle different from the one we are currently living.

They're Just Not Like Us!

All of us know that it is not right to negatively judge other people's actions, values, likes, and dislikes when they don't injure or affect anyone else. But we also know how difficult it is to practice this concept. It is particularly difficult when we have moved away from our parent's values and have chosen a lifestyle of our own. Most of us are living a certain lifestyle because we decided what was best for us, based on our conclusion of what life should be. Many values are identical at various levels in the game. These common values keep society together. They are the glue that allows any society to come together when a crisis occurs. In the American society, these basic values include such things as work ethic, family values, community service, education, and patriotism. This could not be more clearly displayed than the uniting of America after the terrorist bombing of September 11, 2001. The bombing of Pearl Harbor and the assassination of President Kennedy brought similar peaks in unity and patriotism.

Value differences and separations become more apparent, depending on the amount of emphasis we place on any specific basic value. Let's look at how some of these differences affect our attitudes about each other. To begin, there are seven levels on the game board. Level seven is the highest and level three is entry level into our organizations. The socio-economic label for level seven is "Old Money" and for level three it is "Working Class."

Regarding the family unit and raising children, the working class will defend the role of the family as being one of the most important in life. The sentiment is "As goes the family . . . so goes the society!" Level three will most likely tell you that level seven people don't care about their children. As soon as a child is old enough, level sevens send their children away to boarding and/or prep school just so they can "go gallivanting around the world." This is used as clear evidence according to level three standards that people in level seven don't care about their kids or the family unit.

Level seven, on the other hand, cannot quite understand the values of level three. "You know what life is about," says level seven. "It is about making a lasting contribution; leaving a footprint in the sands of time; making a difference for mankind." The Mellon Museum, the Carnegie Library, the Rockefeller Foundation; "giving something back is what life is about." "Level three," says level seven, "could care less about mankind. All they care about is protecting a very small unit called the family. They will not expose their children to a broader concept simply because they cannot see the big picture."

Neither of these attitudes is incorrect, illegal, or immoral; they merely explain the different perspectives held by both groups. We have hinted at a major difference in values between level seven and their level six neighbors. With regard to money, level six is on an endless quest to get as much as they possibly can. Some of the wealthiest people in our country reside at level six. They include such players as Donald Trump, Ted Turner, and Bill Gates, to name a few. At this level, the play is fiercely competitive, with money being the specific reward of good playing. To make as much money as possible is a strong value. Level seven does not place the same value on accumulating wealth. They have enough money to do anything they want; however, they expend considerable effort in "giving back" much of their hard-earned dollars. This is represented by vehicles we have mentioned before, such as the Ford and Rockefeller Foundations and the Mellon Museum. Returning some of the wealth to society as well as pursuing activities that are more charitable are quite natural for the children of level seven members. Since the competitive nature of level six often prevents individuals from reversing their values in their lifetime, the task often falls to the children of first generation wealth. "New money" versus "old money" are terms sometimes used to describe this transition. All of us grew up with certain messages we held as truths. The degree to which we are willing to alter these truths to include other truths will define our ascension up the game board.

Why Do I Always Have to Be the One to Change?

All things are in a constant state of change. It is the only way an individual, organization, or society can survive. Remember, as Will Rogers said, "When you're through changing, you're through!" The problem with this scenario is that although everything is constantly changing, these changes happen at different rates of speed. For example:

Speed of Change

Individual	Organizations	Society
1–3 years	10–30 years	35–100 years

Individual Change: Requires One to Three Years

Individuals can change their values in a relatively short period of time, anywhere from months to several years. The length of time is based on the perceived benefits to the individual— which creates the motivational level leading to action. Also, with the individual, there is no one else to convince, and progress is not hampered by other people dragging their feet. This is an area where we have total control.

Organizational Change: Requires Ten to Thirty Years

The general rule is the larger the body of people, the slower change will occur. An organization of five hundred people can make a value change much faster than an AT&T, IBM, or a large government agency. We have seen time and money spent on current value changes in the area of quality, customer service and diversity in large organizations. Just because a memo from the president's office heralds the impending change does not mean it will happen overnight. Constant management attention, new reward systems, and an endless amount of training and communications are all necessary if true change is to happen. For example, it is not uncommon to hear that "nothing has changed" five years after the announcement of a new effort in an organization. The effort might be progressing but at a speed that is not always apparent. The organization *is* changing but can *you* afford to wait?

Societal Change: Requires Thirty-five to One Hundred Years

This is the slowest of all change. Witnessing two riots in the Los Angeles Watts district, over two decades apart, with basically the same issues at stake, highlights the slowness of societal change. Another example is that it has taken over forty years for our society to shift back to the more conservative Republican party in Congress. The debate over free choice or right to life, school prayer, and capital punishment are issues we know will not be resolved quickly.

The different rates of change impose a dilemma for all of us. It forces us to make more choices. "Can my career wait fifteen years for my company to change values, or should I change my individual values to those of the company and enjoy the rewards much sooner?" This is a question that boils down to how fast do I want my "fast track" career to go, and can I live with the required changes?

It Just Isn't Worth It!

One of the most important aspects of a pyramid structure is to establish the dynamics of competition. To go from the broad base at entry level to one individual or group at the top suggests that somehow, people must be eliminated. This is the competitive nature of a hierarchical structure. A personal example involves my daughter, Kellie, who is now pursuing her career. Early in her school career she wanted to be the best cheerleader that ever performed on a field. To achieve this, she started at an early age and dedicated herself to reaching this goal. Gaining experience in the Colt football leagues and then in junior high school, she continued to develop her skills and knowledge with a zest anyone would admire. Many nights she had to be called into the house after dark from a practice session she and a few friends were having in the backyard. However, the constant practice of her handsprings, splits, and jumps eventually paid off. In her senior year in high school, she was captain of the cheerleading squad that won the state championship. This was just the beginning of her dream. The next step involved becoming a cheerleader for the state university she was going to attend.

A month after she enrolled in college, it was on her first trip home that we had a chance to talk. I was anxious to hear how her quest for the state university's squad was going. I knew that with her skills and desire, stardom was not far off! However, our discussion about cheerleading was a very short one. I asked, "How is cheerleading going?" Kellie told me that she had resigned from the squad a few days before coming home. "Why?" I asked, stunned at the news. "You really wanted to make the team!" "Yeah, I did," she explained, "but in order to be on the team, you had to get up at five-thirty in the morning to go to weight lifting, then to a tumbling class, and after your required classes, you had to spend the rest of the evening practicing." Then came the statement that put it all in perspective for me. "And you know Dad, with all the things to do on campus—it just wasn't worth it to me."

What Kellie had done is what all of us must do if we are honest with ourselves. That is to look at the next level on the pyramid and determine if the dues we must pay at the next level are worth the rewards we will receive once we get to that level. If the answer is "no," because the rewards are not sufficient, then we have made a choice to be happy (at least for the moment) at our current level. When we don't make those choices, we live our lives through outdated dreams and become frustrated, disappointed, and even angry—not only with ourselves but with the world as well.

Our system suggests that to advance, you must pay some dues. You might pay them now or you might pay them later—but *you must pay your dues!* If the dues to obtain the next level are too much for you, you have made a decision to contribute at your current level and, as a result, should be happy. Always remember—it is *your* choice!

How the System Works

Let's take a look at how the system works. Although there are seven levels or leagues in our society, only five fall within the boundaries of organizations. For explanation purposes, let's assign symbols to these five leagues that represent not only job functions but also the corresponding value systems. The game board would then look like this.

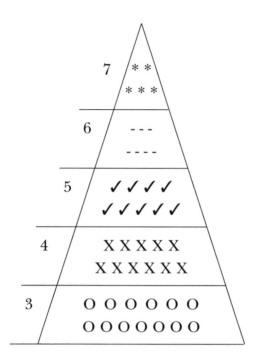

One basic principle of the game is that you must be pulled through the system by someone from a higher level—an individual must become your sponsor. One of the first criteria a sponsor looks for is whether the player has developed a comfort level with the group at the next level. In other words, if the player is placed into the next level, would he or she fit? To place an "O" into a job that requires the values of an "X" would be risky. The equivalent would be to put someone who does not speak French in charge of a French-speaking company. Even though the person might be technically qualified, his inability to communicate within the organization would make him ineffective. The individual would be regarded as a "token" (someone placed in a position for reasons other than his or her qualifications) and would be powerless.

The risk to the sponsor is having to explain to others why he championed an unqualified individual. If this happens too often, the sponsor's ability to read people will be questioned.

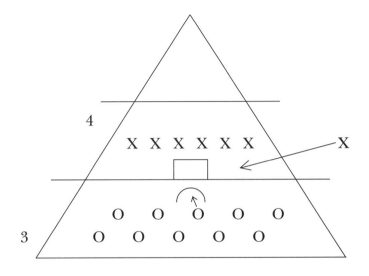

In the illustration above, the circle candidate may be fifty-one years old with twenty-seven years of programming experience. However, since he might not effectively communicate with the other "X's" at the next level, he is unqualified for the job, or is at least a risk. If no other "O" in the organization shows the ability or willingness to become fluent in language "X," then an "X" must be brought in from the outside. This new person is usually called an intern or management trainee.

It is still possible for the fifty-one-year-old "O" to qualify himself by simply learning about and becoming comfortable with the "X" values. As discussed earlier in the chapter, this change may be accomplished in a relatively short period of time—one to three years.

You Can't Go Home Again!

One of the biggest obstacles in choosing to change levels is the realization that you must leave some people behind. This does not mean that you break all contact with old friends and acquaintances, but it usually means that those relationships will change forever.

If you doubt that you do leave people behind, go back to your old neighborhood where your best friend from high school still lives. The first night of your visit will be filled with joyous fellowship as you relive all of the great events and escapades of the "good old days." That evening you will feel that nothing has changed and that your relationship with your friend is as strong as ever. The second evening, upon meeting your friend, you might find more silent moments, simply because most of the common experiences have been covered. As you begin to explain some of your current work and lifestyle experiences, your friend becomes quiet and introspective. You may conclude that the lack of participation by your friend means boredom or resentment because you are bragging about all your accomplishments. Of course, you weren't bragging—just merely talking about the normal challenges in your current life. You listen again to what is going on in the old neighborhood, but nothing much has changed. If you had scheduled an appointment to meet your friend on the third day of your visit, it is quite likely you might find some reason to cancel. This is not because you don't like your old friend, but because you no longer have very much in common. You have learned a new language and a new culture that your old friend does not understand nor to which he can relate. What happened with your old friend was nothing more than the application of another rule: *YOU CAN'T GO HOME AGAIN!* You can visit, you can go home to help, you can go home to express your continued love, but you can't stay. Your value system has changed.

This dynamic is so strong that even a person's family could be affected. It is usually possible to distinguish every working-class cousin from every professional cousin by three o'clock on the day of a family reunion. This is easy to do because by the end of the day they will break into two visible groups. Even the thick bonds of family cannot always overcome cultural or class differences.

The ultimate illustration occurs in a marriage. If one mate grows to another level and the other remains at the initial level when they met, the communication between the two is severely strained. If common interest in activities and lifestyle is not maintained, soon the two become incompatible and divorce is very likely. However, the union is safer as long as there is at least one major common interest—such as children. But we have seen all too often that when the children leave home, the marriage breaks up if no other common interests remain or are identified.

To prevent this from happening, it is important when growing to be a mentor to your mate to ensure that he or she becomes a part of your future lifestyle. To choose a higher lifestyle without the buy-in of your personal support team could have grave consequences.

Hitting the Glass Ceiling

Much has been written recently about the "glass ceiling" in organizations. This is the level in the organization where people with visible differences (such as women and members of minority groups) from majority males have seen their career mobility stopped. There are invisible ceilings for all energetic players, where even the greatest performance results will not allow passage. To better understand the glass ceiling concept, it is important to note that there is more than one.

The first glass ceiling in the organization separates level three from level four. This is the level between non-exempt and exempt positions. We don't think about this ceiling very often because we are very open in explaining how a person can break through.

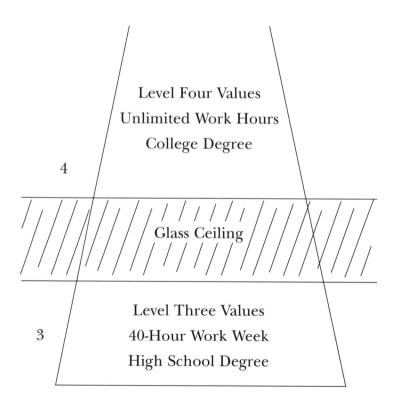

As the illustration above points out, among the more important criteria to move to level four is a college degree and the understanding that payment is not by the hour. These requirements are well publicized, and almost all who are looking for level four responsibilities know that, at a minimum, these two requirements must be met. Because this knowledge is so widespread, people do not talk about the ceiling between three and four. We normally write it off as the choices people make. Do I go to college or do I work after high school graduation? What isn't discussed openly are the value and lifestyle changes that occur between these two levels. In this chapter we will examine those differences in detail.

It is the glass ceiling between levels four and five that is more difficult to understand. Even though a college degree is required, a graduate degree could make a difference. The subtleties of the two cultures sometimes prevents a player from seeing the change in requirements. The reasons for all the discussion of the glass ceiling at this level is two-fold:

1. This is where the visibly different population gets stuck in the organization, with only a few women and minorities being able to break through.

2. We do not openly talk about the change in requirements, and so it is not considered a matter of individual choice (like going to college between levels three and four). As a result, white males, who hold the majority of positions in levels five, six, and seven, are often blamed for the lack of advancement of women and minorities to senior management.

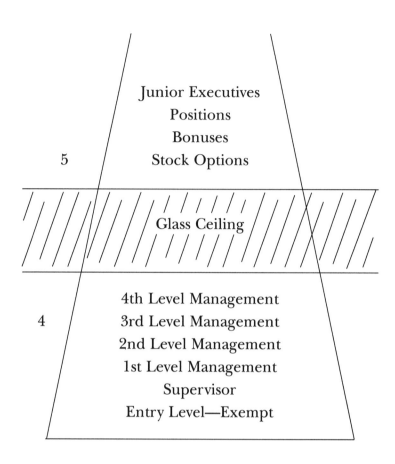

Junior Executives
Positions
Bonuses
5   Stock Options

Glass Ceiling

4th Level Management
4   3rd Level Management
2nd Level Management
1st Level Management
Supervisor
Entry Level—Exempt

Two things can be concluded in the above illustration. First, level four has extensive growth for any player. You can be a fourth level manager in an organization and possibly never have had to alter cultures if you began as an exempt worker. This is deceiving. In the twenty to thirty years it might have taken to get to that fourth level of management, few would believe that the person didn't know the company and its value system. But in reality, that person has grown, while experiencing only a slight change in culture and values. The second step into level five represents one of the bigger cultural changes. This is where the decision is made to sponsor someone into the executive decision-making process for life. These positions, of course, vary with the organization. In the military it is obtaining your first star, in a law firm it is making partner, and in the government it is the first senior executive service position. If someone is not on board with the executive team and its value system, at that level, considerable damage could be done not only to the individual, but to the overall mission of the organization.

Many of the value changes between levels four and five will be discussed in the following chapter, but one of the most obvious is socialization. Level five positions become very visible, and individuals are expected to represent the organization externally in the communities in which they reside. Internal technical skills are not the only requirements that determine qualifications—the executive language and culture must be spoken at this level. It is fair to say that the system is hesitant to promote a woman executive or a black executive to level five. However, it is equally hesitant to promote an Irish, Polish, or Italian executive to level five. The system, however, has little problem in promoting any *executive* that happens to be Irish or any *executive* that happens to be a woman or happens to be black. Colin Powell, as an example, was not an African-American general, he was a general. Every general has to be something else—his background just happens to be African-American. No matter how good he was technically, if he didn't fit into the executive culture, he would not have been able to function effectively in his job. As a matter of fact, the lack of executive fluency is the major reason most players, white or black, male or female, do not reach their executive career objectives. Maybe you have heard a friend or fellow employee say "I do my job, why do I have to be bothered by all this other stuff they ask for?" Well that "other stuff" may be a part of the culture on that level, and anyone not displaying a comfort level or a desire to practice what is required would be considered ineffective. Elements of any level's culture might include such things as appearance, socializing, common interests, and hobbies. Of course, the willingness of a person to fit into the next league is up to each individual—these cultures can be learned rather quickly (one to three years). The ability to move into the next level is dependent upon securing a sponsor who will pull that person to that next level when they see a potential mentee speaking the higher language.

The natural tendency is to mentor and sponsor those individuals with whom we are most comfortable. In the past, since most people at level five or level six were men with European backgrounds, most individuals being mentored were other men with European backgrounds. As a result, many potential young executives were locked out of executive positions because they did not receive the information necessary for continued growth. Today, most forward-thinking executive teams realize that, in this age of diversity, they must force the mentoring process beyond the comfort zone of their executive staff. Since it is not happening naturally, organizations are installing formal mentoring programs. In these programs, women and minorities are being assigned to various executives to better ensure broader mentoring.

This formal process is generally not as effective as the natural "good chemistry" process. However, until the current executive teams become more comfortable with diverse individuals or become more diverse themselves, it is the best solution available.

"No matter what accomplishments you make, somebody helps you."

Wilma Rudolph

"When you're through changing, you're through!"

Will Rogers

"Change is the law of life. Those who always look to the past or present will always miss the future."

John Kennedy

"Dues, you pay them now or you pay them later, but they must be paid."

"It's who you know and who knows you, favorably."

"Once you gain entrance into a lifestyle, you will be given the means with which to stay."

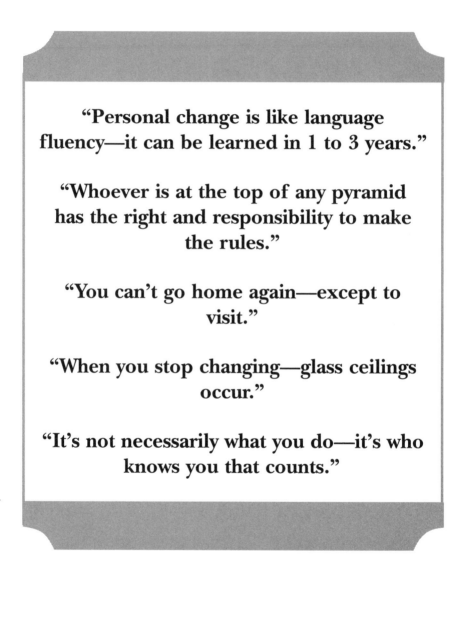

"Personal change is like language fluency—it can be learned in 1 to 3 years."

"Whoever is at the top of any pyramid has the right and responsibility to make the rules."

"You can't go home again—except to visit."

"When you stop changing—glass ceilings occur."

"It's not necessarily what you do—it's who knows you that counts."

CHAPTER 6

The Game Board

In Chapter Five we used symbols (O, X, ✓, -, *) to represent various leagues on the game board. In this chapter we now want to replace those symbols with some of the specific lifestyle elements that define the culture of each level. It is important to remember that this information is to serve as a model or guide, and is therefore not all inclusive. Activities and elements may differ from community to community. Also note that many of your personal activities extend over several different leagues. This is not unusual. Take a close look at the league that holds some of the newer activities you are engaged in, because this may suggest a personal transition for you. All pyramids do not apply to everyone, but overall, you should be able to determine your current level. Let's look at the seven leagues of the game board and their major elements.

The dynamics of the pyramid indicate that those at the top make the rules. However, it is important to recognize that there are pyramids within pyramids within pyramids:

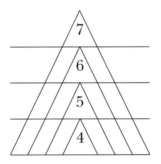

If this is the case, and I am at the top of pyramid "4," I can set the rules over the smaller pyramid "4" as long as those rules do not conflict with any of the rules established by pyramid "5." This hierarchical structure continues until we reach pyramid "7," which sets the rules for the entire structure. In government, this is called the federal system, with the federal government being able to overrule any state law if it is in conflict with federal law. The same is true with corporate, military, and even religious institutions. Even though the parish priest operates autonomously, it is the Vatican that sets the ultimate direction for the Catholic church.

Who's at the Top?

Because there are many different pyramids in the system, many different communities have an influence in making the rules by which we live. The ultimate rule-maker in our lives is the federal government. Although the American government allows other entities to exist freely, everyone understands that when any interest is in conflict with the well-being of the whole society, the federal government will prevail. The government takeover of industry during World War II is a good example. Since most of our waking hours are spent at work, the majority of the rules we live by in our system comes from four entities:

- Government (federal, state, and/or local);
- Board of directors (private or public);
- Commissions (e.g., SEC, FCC);
- Agencies (e.g., FAA, EPA).

In reality, a person cannot drive a city block, plug in a toaster, or work in a profession without some law or regulation affecting that activity.

To define your current level or the level to which you might want to advance, we must look at the lifestyle displayed at each level. Even though very few will do all things at any given level, many individuals will be connected with enough activities to eventually be associated with belonging to that level. For instance, there is a very definite relationship between level seven behavior and lifestyle (the highest level) in the socio-economic class level, and that of one's position (executive), education (Ivy League), automobile (Mercedes), and leisure activities (polo, patron of the arts). This is not to say that people in the lower socio-economic levels never will purchase a Mercedes—or enjoy the ballet—they do—however, level seven's lifestyle is a pattern of behavior including many activities, not just a car.

So what? Why do these things matter? Well, if one is to advance in the organization, especially toward the top of the pyramid verses horizonal movement, one is expected to function at that level in many aspects of one's life. All of us want our executives to promote the organization within the community. We expect them, by their positive association with other corporate executives, to at least give our company an opportunity for additional business and a more enhanced reputation.

People usually do business with people they like or at least with whom they are comfortable. This is why top executives tend to live in the same areas, congregate at the same social organizations and clubs, and promote the same charitable activities.

If one is fluent in the language of level six or level seven, chances are he/she will be comfortable discussing the stock market, the dollar, current events, politics, the theatre, the symphony, history, and other topics. They must take an active role in local charities, drive a late model luxury car, play golf and/or tennis at one of the more accepted country clubs, have a passing knowledge of fine wine, dine at the better restaurants, and so on.

So you can see that there is a great deal more to being an executive than simply excelling in your chosen profession. The intrusion into one's time and privacy is offensive to many and is undoubtedly the reason many plateau at a lower level in the organization.

Still, for those who are willing to pay the price for corporate success, a knowledge of the game (and understanding of the price) is invaluable. In this chapter we will review the following in detail:

- Occupation
- Where People Live
- Location of Home
- Entertaining in the Home
- Money
- Leisure Activities
- Fine Arts
- Cars
- Vacation Choices

As mentioned earlier, this information is not all inclusive, but should give you a clear idea of many of the elements within each league or level.

OCCUPATION

LEVEL SEVEN

Many groups share level seven's rule-making responsibilities. Business players, among several others, have a dominant role in level seven activities. The most powerful in this category are the older families of wealthy tycoons such as DuPont, Mellon, Astor, and Rockefeller. Many are not as wealthy as many of the level six players, but their money has been around for several generations, and as a result, they have created a strong power base—thus the term "old money." Among others joining these families are the Boards of Directors of the top twenty industrial organizations, the top ten banks in the country, the most prestigious Wall Street law firms and brokerage houses, as well as the top ten insurance companies.

Other groups represented in level seven include top leaders in government, education, the military, non-profit organizations, and the fine arts. The president of the United States and his major appointees including cabinet members, Supreme Court justices, major ambassadors, the Joint Chiefs of Staff, major commission heads, among others, also occupy this level. Political power often proves to be the ultimate power in our system; however, it is short lived. In our democratic system, the Office of the President holds the power, not the individual in the office. Upon leaving the office, the individual must return to his level of fluency. For example, upon leaving office, former President Carter returned to Georgia and former President Reagan returned to California to level six environments. Had President Roosevelt and President Kennedy not died in office, they would have returned to their level seven environments.

LEVEL SIX

This level contains the second most influential group in the game. It is the level of the game that moves from national to regional prominence. Influence in various regions comes from those who hold the positions of governor, senator (without major committee responsibilities), Board of Director members of the Fortune 1,000 firms (verses top 50), as well as some corporate and divisional heads of the major top twenty industrials. The "Jet Set" crowd may also be found at level six. This includes the top movie stars, sports figures, and stars in television and music. Also at this level are those people who have made tremendous fortunes with their efforts. People like Ted Turner, Sam Walton, Donald Trump, Ross Perot, and Bill Gates might be good examples of the "new money" that is emerging.

LEVEL FIVE

Members at this level serve dual roles. On the one hand, it is the point at which serious game players begin to emerge—those in middle management positions, small business owners, and others. On the other hand, those who choose to be experts in their field tend to level off here. A prerequisite for anyone to advance into level six or seven is the ability to delegate the details of their work, which is one of the major skills of the game. Obviously, airline pilots, surgeons, and other experts on this level must perform their duties themselves, so delegation is not an option. In order for these people to advance beyond level five, they must consider administrative and executive positions, which require getting things done directly through other people.

LEVEL FOUR

Level four is often called the professional or "White Collar" class. It includes salespeople, accountants, engineers, programmers, systems analysts, and craft workers such as carpenters and plumbers. It also includes Fortune 500 managers and their equals in education, government, and the military. Fluctuating one level in either direction can happen, depending upon individual fluency and the size of a particular company or organization.

LEVEL THREE

This level includes support and administrative personnel and individuals working at plant locations or in construction. As our society moves toward a service economy, additional occupations are being added to this level.

LEVEL TWO

Part-time workers are found on this level, usually working at minimum wage. This includes small farmers, students, and homemakers, who have a limited amount of time to put toward an external occupation.

LEVEL ONE

Level one contains people who have dropped out of the system. This includes street and homeless people and those who are permanently unemployable.

The following illustration shows the occupations identified and their location on the game board.

LEVEL COMPOSITE

L E V E L S

7
- OFFICE OF THE U.S. PRESIDENT AND MAJOR APPOINTEES
- OLDER LARGE FAMILY BUSINESSES
- BOARDS OF TOP 20 INDUSTRIALS AND TOP 10 BANKS
- WALL STREET LAW FIRMS, INSURANCE COMPANIES, ETC.
- NATIONAL LEGISLATORS AND MAJOR COMMITTEE HEADS

6
- EXECUTIVE MANAGERS IN LARGE CORPORATIONS
- MILITARY CHIEFS OF STAFF
- JET SET INTERNATIONAL ENTERTAINERS AND SPORTS FIGURES
- GOVERNORS, MOST OF THE NATIONAL LEGISLATURE
- GENERAL MANAGERS IN LARGE CORPORATIONS

5
- MIDDLE MANAGERS IN LARGE CORPORATIONS
- EXPERTS IN THEIR FIELDS (e.g., DOCTORS, LAWYERS, RESEARCHERS)
- MEDIUM- TO LARGE-SCALE FARMERS
- SMALL BUSINESS OWNERS

4
- 1ST–4TH LEVEL MANAGEMENT IN LARGE CORPORATIONS
- PROFESSIONAL OR SALARIED EMPLOYEES (e.g., SALESPERSONS, ENGINEERS, TEACHERS, PLANT SUPERVISORS)

3
- SUPPORT AND ADMINISTRATION WORKERS
- HOURLY EMPLOYEES (e.g., MANUFACTURING, CONSTRUCTION)

2
- SMALL FARMERS
- PART-TIME MINIMUM WAGE EARNERS

1
- PERMANENTLY UNEMPLOYABLE
- STREET AND HOMELESS PEOPLE

OCCUPATION

Pyramids within Pyramids

Every occupation has a pyramidal structure of its own. For that reason, it is all the more important that there be common elements at each level to allow the different occupations to communicate with each other. As an example, the business, military, government, education, and political leaders in any city will have common interests in social and cultural affairs that will bring them all together. Without these common elements, they would have to operate in a vacuum.

Lifestyle, the Glue of the System

Once the occupational pyramids are in place, a common value system is necessary to allow effective interaction among the various occupations. Those common elements are known as lifestyle activities. Some of these lifestyle elements are examined in greater detail on the following pages.

WHERE PEOPLE LIVE

Growing up, my mother used to say, "You are who you hang around with." To some degree that also applies to people we live, work, and play around. We are a nation of communities, and these communities are defined by parameters such as socio-economic level, ethnicity, race, sexual orientation, age, occupation, and religion. Many individuals strengthen comfort zones by combining several of the communities into one. It is not unusual to find neighborhoods of older, professional Jewish individuals or one of working-class Irish Catholic, union workers in any given city.

LEVEL SEVEN

There are thirteen cities in the United States that operate at level seven. Eleven of these cities are located in the northeastern part of the country and publish a social register. There are no southern cities with a social register, and the only level seven city west of the Mississippi River is San Francisco. The other twelve cities are: New York, Boston, Philadelphia, Pittsburgh, Dayton, Wilmington (known as the DuPont Register), Chicago, Cleveland, St. Louis, Cincinnati, Buffalo, and Baltimore. These cities represent much of the power of the business community and are primarily the locations for headquarter operations for the Fortune 500 companies. The social register is a gathering of old money families who create a social network for themselves and their children, as well as take on the responsibility of supporting the fine arts. As a result, these cities have the best symphonies, ballet/opera companies, and museums in the country. The greatest rule-making city in our society is, of course, Washington, D.C. (home of our federal government); but it has a four-year turnover and thus lacks the stability for a permanent social register. There is, however, a document called "The Green Book," which publishes the names of the Washington, D.C. elite after every election. In recent years the individual city social registers have been combined into one national register.

LEVEL SIX

Many of the emerging southern cities fall into this category. They include cities such as Atlanta, Miami, Houston, Phoenix, and Dallas. Other cities include Denver, Seattle, and Los Angeles. These are the cities that provide regional leadership to our country.

LEVEL FIVE

Level five is the location for many developing cities such as Tampa, New Orleans, Orlando, Jacksonville, and Charlotte. The major factors that separate these cities from those of level six are the number of divisional and regional offices of major corporations located there, the funding levels of their cultural arts programs, and their ability to attract major sports franchises. Many of these locations formed regional artistic companies in the areas of music and dance, which allows citizens of that region to enjoy the fine arts.

LEVEL FOUR

Many of the small industrial cities are found in level four. These are the cities that will have regional rather than national recognition. These cities may gain importance by being the center for a major university or the state capital. They include cities such as Columbus, OH, Sacramento, CA, and Harrisburg, PA.

LEVEL THREE

Level three embraces the small towns. They will usually have a quantity of large manufacturing plants and a substantial service industry base. Locations such as Peoria, IL, Macon, GA, and New Castle, PA, may be included in this level.

LEVEL TWO

Smaller farming communities or small manufacturing locations may be found at this level.

LEVEL ONE

Undeveloped rural areas in the country, where very few people live may be found at this level.

LEVEL COMPOSITE

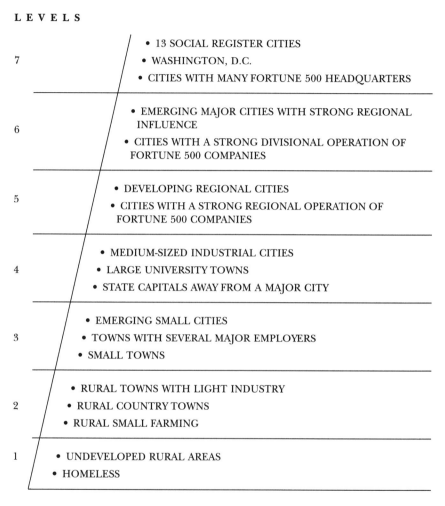

L E V E L S

7
- 13 SOCIAL REGISTER CITIES
- WASHINGTON, D.C.
- CITIES WITH MANY FORTUNE 500 HEADQUARTERS

6
- EMERGING MAJOR CITIES WITH STRONG REGIONAL INFLUENCE
- CITIES WITH A STRONG DIVISIONAL OPERATION OF FORTUNE 500 COMPANIES

5
- DEVELOPING REGIONAL CITIES
- CITIES WITH A STRONG REGIONAL OPERATION OF FORTUNE 500 COMPANIES

4
- MEDIUM-SIZED INDUSTRIAL CITIES
- LARGE UNIVERSITY TOWNS
- STATE CAPITALS AWAY FROM A MAJOR CITY

3
- EMERGING SMALL CITIES
- TOWNS WITH SEVERAL MAJOR EMPLOYERS
- SMALL TOWNS

2
- RURAL TOWNS WITH LIGHT INDUSTRY
- RURAL COUNTRY TOWNS
- RURAL SMALL FARMING

1
- UNDEVELOPED RURAL AREAS
- HOMELESS

WHERE PEOPLE LIVE

LOCATION OF HOME

The location of your home in the city where you live is another choice and another pyramid. The possible break-down of these seven levels are as follows.

LEVEL SEVEN

People at this level generally have a home in one of the social register cities, as well as other homes elsewhere in the country. Residences may also be found outside of the United States.

LEVEL SIX

Generally, individuals own homes in the more exclusive areas of the city. Frequently, the homes are custom built and have private swimming pools and tennis court facilities.

LEVEL FIVE

These individuals usually own homes in country club neighborhoods with easy access to swimming pools, tennis courts, and other leisure activities. These areas may also include newly renovated homes in various upscale neighborhoods.

LEVEL FOUR

Development or tract homes in suburban communities are in this league. The purchase and renovation of older in-town properties are frequently found at this level, as well as upscale condominiums.

LEVEL THREE

Individuals experience the "American Dream" in this league—owning their first home. Many at this level will live in rental properties and might choose to reside in ethnic communities. These ethnic communities are clearly identified, like Chinatown, Germantown, Little Italy, or the Black community.

LEVEL TWO

Dwellings in rural areas are found here as well as rent-subsidized properties. The inner city housing project communities are included in this league as well. This is often a temporary stay for some, but for others it is permanent.

LEVEL ONE

Individuals in this level may live with others, in some instances by choice, in other instances by circumstance. Many are homeless.

LEVEL COMPOSITE

LEVELS

7
- EXCLUSIVE HOME IN ONE OF THE SOCIAL REGISTER CITIES
- MANSIONS IN TOP CITIES/MOST EXCLUSIVE AREA OF TOWN
- HAVE ADDITIONAL HOMES IN SEVERAL LOCATIONS OF THE COUNTRY

6
- EXCLUSIVE AREAS IN THE CITY
- HOMES ARE OFTEN CUSTOM BUILT WITH PRIVATE TENNIS COURTS AND SWIMMING POOLS

5
- COUNTRY CLUB NEIGHBORHOODS WITH TENNIS/ SWIM CLUBS AVAILABLE
- REVITALIZED UPPER MIDDLE CLASS COMMUNITIES IN MAJOR CITIES

4
- SUBURBAN COMMUNITIES—DEVELOPMENT OR TRACT HOUSES
- REHABILITATION OF OLDER IN-TOWN PROPERTY (OFTEN YOUNG PROFESSIONALS)
- OWNERSHIP OF IN-TOWN PROPERTY (TOWN-HOUSE)

3
- OWNERSHIP OF FIRST HOME (THE "AMERICAN DREAM")
- RENTING IN DOWNTOWN AREAS OF LARGE CITIES
- ETHNIC COMMUNITIES; FRINGE AREAS OF LARGE CITIES

2
- DEPRESSED RURAL AREAS
- INNER CITY IN RENT-SUBSIDIZED PROPERTY
- INNER CITY HOUSING PROJECT COMMUNITIES

1
- DO NOT HAVE A HOME

LOCATION OF HOME

ENTERTAINING IN THE HOME

Entertaining in one's home is a crucial aspect of any culture or level and is a constant reminder that the game is about people.

LEVELS SIX AND SEVEN

At upper level cocktail parties, people are constantly working as they circulate among the guests. Although social interchange happens at these affairs, the main purpose is to gain exposure and increase the comfort level of old and new networks. Malcolm Forbes, former head of the Forbes business empire and once noted for elaborate parties aboard his yacht, was reported to have said, "If anyone comes to one of my parties and doesn't know that they are working, they probably shouldn't be here!" This is strong evidence that, whereas people in lower leagues socialize to have "fun," higher league players socialize to affect moves on the game board. For the serious player, "having fun" is secondary; however, making some effective moves and/or gaining important contacts can be fun as well, if you are mentally into the game.

At a typical upper league party, it might be possible to meet twenty-five people, hand out ten business cards, have three lunches as a result, and close one or two business deals . . . pretty good production for one evening's work! The president of the United States might go to three formal dinner parties in one week, but sitting beside him will be another president, prime minister, or premier. The environment will be very festive, but he will be working every night, including many Saturdays.

Once people meet you, accept you, and feel you can deliver satisfactorily on the product or service, they will give you their business. This is called sponsorship. Knocking on doors is the toughest way to sell. If you meet people socially, they might give you business you didn't expect and can then introduce you to all of their friends as well.

LEVEL FIVE

A major transition in the game occurs at level five. At this level, the game becomes more serious than the levels below, demanding a blend of social and business life. It's the point at which the boss is invited, whether liked or not, simply because it is politically astute to do so.

Your presence at these parties is vital. Whenever you hear someone say, "I work with those people all week. I'm certainly not going to spend Saturday night with them, too!" they are sending a strong message that they're not interested in playing in the upper levels. If you are interested in upward mobility and do not actively participate in social events, you may not be considered a serious player. It's no surprise that we see the serious game players emerge at this stage.

If you carefully watch people operate at this level, you can see how these players establish contacts who will be assets and eliminate those who will not. Conversations in this environment are geared to determine where a person ranks in the league structure. A typical conversation may flow like this:

"I see by your name tag that your name is Bill Johnson. How are you doing? My name is Jim Smith. Who are you with, Bill (organization/company)? What do you do with them (position/function)?"

After he answers Jim's questions, it's Bill's turn to ask the same of Jim. This will definitely be a two-way probing session.

Jim continues, "Mike and Mona have a lovely home! Are you neighbors? Do you live around here? Oh. Where do you live?" (He's probing for the level position that deals with housing. In other words, does Bill live in a level three neighborhood, or a level six like the hosts?)

Jim: "Did you see that last game between Louisville and Duke in the NCAA tournament? Wasn't it great? By the way, where did you go to school? Did you do any graduate studies there?" Bill responds, then rephrases the questions and fires them back at Jim.

Jim probes further: "Do you play tennis or golf? At which club? Ah, yes, beautiful facilities. I belong to the Oak Park Country Club myself." Then Jim pauses while Bill asks the same questions about activities and interests.

This exchange leads to other probes, such as the names of associations with which Bill is affiliated, the corporate boards he might sit on, charitable organizations he advises, and, of course, the role Bill fills with each activity. If the conversation turns to the fine arts, questions would be directed toward discovering the other person's knowledge, interest, and involvement in ballet, opera, theatre, museums, and the symphony.

In less than fifteen minutes, both Bill and Jim can part company with a very good understanding of the level in which the other currently participates. An hour into the party, Jim can scan the room, saying to himself, "That guy over there, he's a 5.38 player. That tall woman is a 6.51. The fellow in the corner is a 6.12, and Jerry . . . well, Jerry's a 4.37 . . . he's in a level below me and can't help me much. But he's a good guy— I might be able to give him some business." (This becomes an act of sponsorship.) For the players who have done this for years, this is not a conscious effort. Most don't even know they are doing it. It has become natural, comfortable, and fun.

We need to keep in mind the fact that business at the upper levels is not a "9 to 5" proposition. Forty-hour work weeks stop with level three play. Upper level business is frequently subtle, much like the opening conversation at the party. The questions we ask in order to develop our score sheet on other players and to qualify our contacts are also crucial in helping us to identify and broaden our business and social networks. Developing relationships both above and below your current level is important—remember, the game is about people, everything else is detail.

LEVELS ONE, TWO, THREE, AND FOUR

If we go from the bottom up with these four categories we must begin at level two, since participants in level one do not entertain. In level two people meet at relatives' homes for holidays and for special occasions. In level three, personal friends are included in casual gatherings such as barbecues. Level four is where cocktail parties begin. A party at this level normally includes only friends—seldom are people from the office involved. If someone *is* invited from work, it is only because that person is a friend. The party will be sporty and informal, with the host often making the hors d'oeuvres and everyone serving themselves at the bar. Normally, very little business is discussed—everyone came to have fun by playing board games, dancing, or joining in a sing-along. In fact, if much business is discussed by any individual at level four parties, they may be excluded from subsequent invitations.

LEVEL COMPOSITE

LEVELS

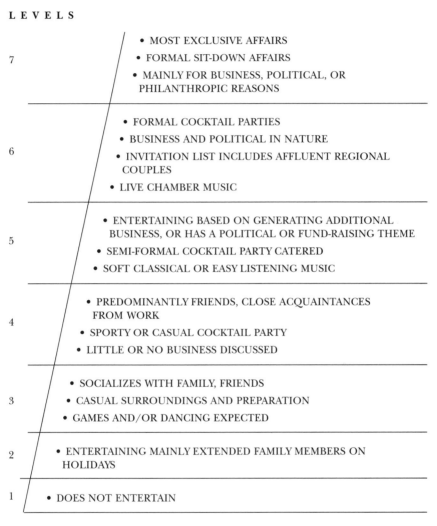

7
- MOST EXCLUSIVE AFFAIRS
- FORMAL SIT-DOWN AFFAIRS
- MAINLY FOR BUSINESS, POLITICAL, OR PHILANTHROPIC REASONS

6
- FORMAL COCKTAIL PARTIES
- BUSINESS AND POLITICAL IN NATURE
- INVITATION LIST INCLUDES AFFLUENT REGIONAL COUPLES
- LIVE CHAMBER MUSIC

5
- ENTERTAINING BASED ON GENERATING ADDITIONAL BUSINESS, OR HAS A POLITICAL OR FUND-RAISING THEME
- SEMI-FORMAL COCKTAIL PARTY CATERED
- SOFT CLASSICAL OR EASY LISTENING MUSIC

4
- PREDOMINANTLY FRIENDS, CLOSE ACQUAINTANCES FROM WORK
- SPORTY OR CASUAL COCKTAIL PARTY
- LITTLE OR NO BUSINESS DISCUSSED

3
- SOCIALIZES WITH FAMILY, FRIENDS
- CASUAL SURROUNDINGS AND PREPARATION
- GAMES AND/OR DANCING EXPECTED

2
- ENTERTAINING MAINLY EXTENDED FAMILY MEMBERS ON HOLIDAYS

1
- DOES NOT ENTERTAIN

ENTERTAINING IN THE HOME

LEISURE ACTIVITIES

When Prince Charles visits the United States, you can bet he doesn't look for a bowling game to pass a few hours. He finds a polo match, because that is one of the sports of his level.

Leisure activities, of course, occur at all levels on the pyramid. This category is difficult to define because people participate in many activities outside of their achieved level. For example, a level three player may play golf, even though golf is normally viewed as a level four through seven activity.

It is important to remember that in any of the categories, exceptions may be found. However, upon closer examination, the majority of individuals who live, work, and enjoy a lifestyle in a particular level will most often conform to the activities associated with that level.

This is a social system, and your leisure activities play an important role. Let's look at golf as an example. By the time you've played fifteen holes, you know the other person, and they are more comfortable with you. By the time you reach the nineteenth hole (the social period after the game), you are well on the way to developing a relationship that will allow you to close the deal if all the performance factors are in line. You were able to have your "day in court," because you had an activity in common that brought you together.

If you aren't adept in the leisure activities of your level, and yet you're serious about the game, then you may want to consider improving and/or developing your skills in order to keep up. How do you do that? Make the commitment. Take bridge or tennis lessons. Go to a golf driving range. Pick up a book or video about the activity. The speed at which you learn the game is determined by your seriousness. You can learn almost all of the leisure activities identified well enough to play socially within a year or less. It really isn't a big deal. Think about it: If you are going to work for the next twenty-five or thirty-five years, the effort is really a very small investment. Dues must be paid if you are to advance. We can very easily categorize these efforts as personal development or self-improvement. Even though it may be work, be careful, you just might have fun learning and participating in those new activities! The field of contestants must be narrowed at the peak of the pyramid. All players will not choose to continue experiencing new activities; thus, this area becomes simply another eliminator in the game.

LEVEL SEVEN

At this level, activities include memberships in elite national clubs that offer immediate access to and participation in exclusive sports and social events. The sports may include fox hunting, polo, and formal dinner parties, which are closed to those who do not "belong" to the group.

LEVEL SIX

Participants here belong to various types of exclusive clubs. Sports and leisure activities may include flying, sailing, yachting, and horse racing. Formal cocktail parties may become one of the more frequent social activities.

LEVEL FIVE

In level five, individuals attend and/or participate in sports events such as golf or tennis. Based on their location and business affiliation, many individuals belong to country clubs and/or luncheon clubs. Socializing at charity functions and business cocktail parties also begins at this level.

LEVEL FOUR

Activities here include skiing, golf, tennis, bridge, and occasional parties. At this level, individuals may experiment with lots of different activities, without putting a great deal of energy into any one.

LEVEL THREE

This level focuses on a large number of family-oriented activities. These may include such things as fishing, hunting, and camping. At the same time, socializing occurs during team sports activities and a lively tavern society.

LEVEL TWO

Family activities are a central focus of this level as well. This may take the form of spending time at home watching television, dancing, playing board or card games, picnics, and other events where family members are included.

LEVEL ONE

Most frequently, individuals here take advantage of activities that are publicly sponsored.

LEVEL COMPOSITE

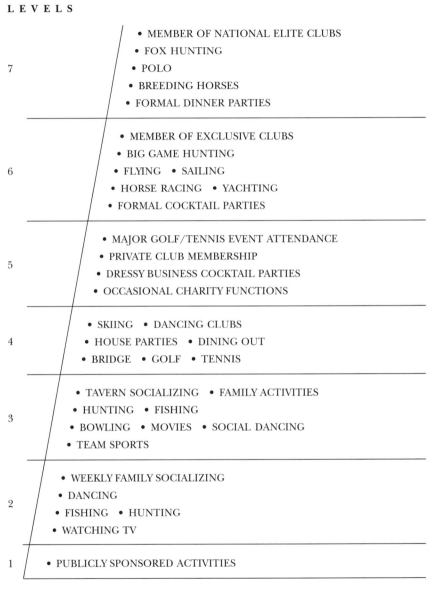

LEVELS

7
- MEMBER OF NATIONAL ELITE CLUBS
- FOX HUNTING
- POLO
- BREEDING HORSES
- FORMAL DINNER PARTIES

6
- MEMBER OF EXCLUSIVE CLUBS
- BIG GAME HUNTING
- FLYING • SAILING
- HORSE RACING • YACHTING
- FORMAL COCKTAIL PARTIES

5
- MAJOR GOLF/TENNIS EVENT ATTENDANCE
- PRIVATE CLUB MEMBERSHIP
- DRESSY BUSINESS COCKTAIL PARTIES
- OCCASIONAL CHARITY FUNCTIONS

4
- SKIING • DANCING CLUBS
- HOUSE PARTIES • DINING OUT
- BRIDGE • GOLF • TENNIS

3
- TAVERN SOCIALIZING • FAMILY ACTIVITIES
- HUNTING • FISHING
- BOWLING • MOVIES • SOCIAL DANCING
- TEAM SPORTS

2
- WEEKLY FAMILY SOCIALIZING
- DANCING
- FISHING • HUNTING
- WATCHING TV

1
- PUBLICLY SPONSORED ACTIVITIES

LEISURE ACTIVITIES

THE FINE ARTS

The Fine Arts arena is one where members of the top two levels return something of lasting value to their communities. In every city with a social register, you will find many of the giant patrons of the arts. Normally the arts are associated with old money from various families. Organizations such as the Rockefeller Foundation in New York, the Andrew Carnegie Museum and Library in Pittsburgh, and the Kennedy Center in Washington, D.C. are all examples of patronage from members in level seven. Because of this patronage, some of these cities have attracted the best artists and musicians in the world.

By level six, individuals are very involved with the arts on a regional or local level. This is evident in emerging cities like Atlanta, Dallas, and Miami. Often, this requires a city to be old enough to have second or third generation business organizations to provide funds in the form of foundation grants or the establishment of trusts. The Robert Woodruff Foundation in Atlanta is a good example. Robert Woodruff, founder of the Coca-Cola empire, helped build the Woodruff Arts Memorial Center, the home of the Atlanta Symphony Orchestra. Additionally, he aided the High Museum of Art and was a large contributor to Emory University as well as numerous other organizations touched by his foundation.

Level six includes a group often called the "Jet Set." This group does not generally operate under conservative corporate America rules, even though they have enough money to function at level six. They are international in scope and activities, and usually travel within their own separate circles.

These circles do not necessarily give them access to the more conservative and established families at this level. Models, movie stars, sports personalities, and rock stars are among those labelled as Jet Setters. Many of our fads and fashions come from this group.

LEVEL SEVEN

The patrons of the arts are found on this level, or individuals who support the symphony, ballet, opera, and visual arts, among others. Their efforts may include attendance as well as financial support for these events and organizations.

LEVEL SIX

At level six, individuals become involved in the international arts activities as well as serving as members of boards and/or trustee groups. Participation includes attendance and some degree of financial support.

LEVEL FIVE

Generally, people at this level are season ticket holders for arts activities in their geographical area. Attendance at showings and performances is often one of the ways support is demonstrated.

LEVEL FOUR

Interest on this level turns primarily toward the theatre. Occasionally, individuals will attend symphony and/or ballet performances.

LEVEL THREE

Since many activities are family-focused on this level, attendance may consist of community and high school productions. Theatre interest is often visible when popular productions tour the country. Movies may also provide a channel to meet the needs of people at this level.

LEVEL TWO

Neither time nor disposable income may be available to individuals at this level. As a result, television is frequently the most accessible vehicle used to enjoy the cultural arts.

LEVEL ONE

Interest may exist for some individuals at this level; however, in the majority of cases, the fine arts may not be financially feasible or accessible.

LEVEL COMPOSITE

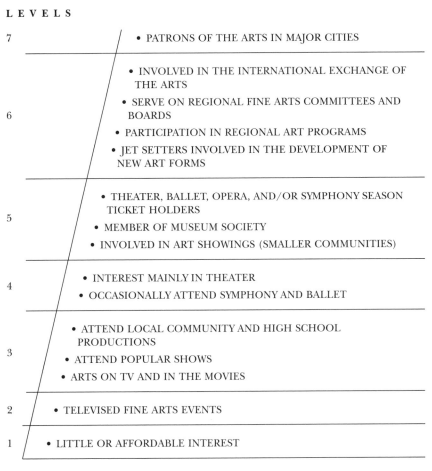

LEVELS

7 • PATRONS OF THE ARTS IN MAJOR CITIES

6
- INVOLVED IN THE INTERNATIONAL EXCHANGE OF THE ARTS
- SERVE ON REGIONAL FINE ARTS COMMITTEES AND BOARDS
- PARTICIPATION IN REGIONAL ART PROGRAMS
- JET SETTERS INVOLVED IN THE DEVELOPMENT OF NEW ART FORMS

5
- THEATER, BALLET, OPERA, AND/OR SYMPHONY SEASON TICKET HOLDERS
- MEMBER OF MUSEUM SOCIETY
- INVOLVED IN ART SHOWINGS (SMALLER COMMUNITIES)

4
- INTEREST MAINLY IN THEATER
- OCCASIONALLY ATTEND SYMPHONY AND BALLET

3
- ATTEND LOCAL COMMUNITY AND HIGH SCHOOL PRODUCTIONS
- ATTEND POPULAR SHOWS
- ARTS ON TV AND IN THE MOVIES

2 • TELEVISED FINE ARTS EVENTS

1 • LITTLE OR AFFORDABLE INTEREST

THE FINE ARTS

CARS

There is truth to the old adage that "you can determine a person's importance by the number of keys he carries!" For instance, a person at level seven will not carry any, for a butler will open the house, an assistant opens the office, and a chauffeur drives the car.

Not too surprisingly, cars also fit into the various levels, just the same as homes and jobs. However, we don't have to look too far to find evidence of people buying outside their level. When we drive through a level three neighborhood and we see a level five car parked on the street, we know intuitively that the owner is trying to buy a position higher on the game board than the rest of his lifestyle dictates. He's not playing by the rules. Level five cars belong in level five neighborhoods. As many business tycoons have experienced, it is very difficult, if not impossible, to buy your way into a higher level.

LEVEL SEVEN

More often, individuals are driven by chauffeurs at this level. Multiple cars and a variety of models and makes are also seen here.

LEVEL SIX

Frequently, very expensive cars and numerous vehicles are found among the "Jet Set" participants. Rolls Royce's and Bentley's are possible examples of the cars at this level.

LEVEL FIVE

The luxury cars are located here. Cars such as Mercedes, Cadillac, Acura, and Lexus are examples of cars owned by level five participants.

LEVEL FOUR

Participants at this level are often owners of a big American car such as a Ford, Buick, or Lincoln. In addition, they may also own a smaller second car. Younger people might purchase vans or mid-sized sport utility vehicles such as Jeeps and Ford Explorers.

LEVEL THREE

Intermediate-sized cars and/or a van and trucks are more often found here. This may connect back to either family activities and/or occupational needs.

LEVEL TWO

Individuals may own an older car and/or a truck. Both vehicles often serve multiple purposes of work and transportation.

LEVEL ONE

In most instances, individuals at this level own no car.

LEVEL COMPOSITE

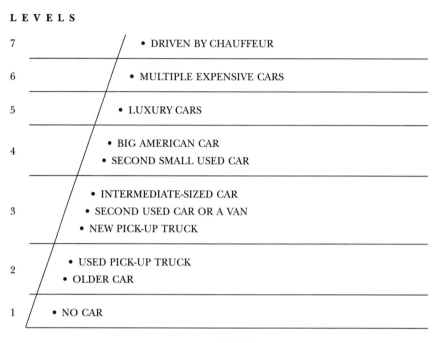

LEVELS

7 • DRIVEN BY CHAUFFEUR

6 • MULTIPLE EXPENSIVE CARS

5 • LUXURY CARS

4 • BIG AMERICAN CAR
  • SECOND SMALL USED CAR

3 • INTERMEDIATE-SIZED CAR
  • SECOND USED CAR OR A VAN
  • NEW PICK-UP TRUCK

2 • USED PICK-UP TRUCK
  • OLDER CAR

1 • NO CAR

CARS

VACATIONS

One of the major molding experiences for children, as they learn the values of their family, is the family vacation. During this period, parents have time to communicate many of their basic values to their children in a relaxing setting. By participating in activities, children become comfortable with a variety of interests. There is also a strong possibility of their continuing these activities into their adult life.

Many factors are taken into account when a family decides where to vacation. These factors may include the amount of money available, interest of the parents, amount of time available, age of the children, and whether or not they own vacation property.

Although all vacations are designed for fun and relaxation, those taken at the upper levels also serve as an opportunity to do some social networking. This happens best by taking repeated vacations to the same location where property might be owned.

LEVEL SEVEN

Extended vacations abroad, sometimes covering months, are more prevalent at this level. This also includes visits to vacation homes in various upscale locations (e.g., Palm Beach, Hyannis Port, St. Moritz).

LEVEL SIX

International travel at least once a year and visits to exclusive resort areas in the United States are among the ways vacation time is spent. At this level, a cruise or a yachting vacation may be considered.

LEVEL FIVE

Individuals at this level may travel regularly to resorts in the United States, take a cruise, go to the beach or mountains, or go skiing as primary vacation activities.

LEVEL FOUR

Individuals most often drive to vacation spots within the country in addition to a visit back to their hometown. On occasion, trips are taken to vacation resorts.

LEVEL THREE

Visits to parents or other out-of-town relatives are frequently made. This is not to suggest that people in other levels do not visit relations or parents; however, at the higher levels they have additional choices available as to how they spend their vacation time.

LEVEL TWO

Participants at this level may stay home on their vacation. Some may not even have a vacation, based on their professional affiliation.

LEVEL ONE

Individuals at this level usually do not take vacations.

LEVEL COMPOSITE

L E V E L S

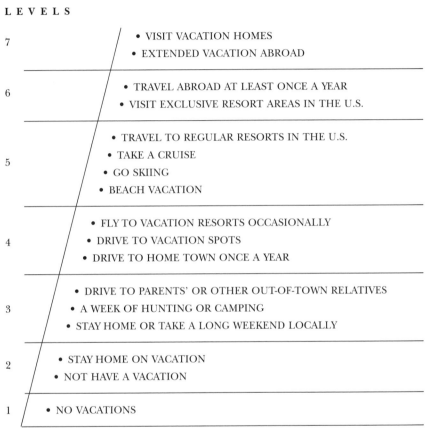

7
- VISIT VACATION HOMES
- EXTENDED VACATION ABROAD

6
- TRAVEL ABROAD AT LEAST ONCE A YEAR
- VISIT EXCLUSIVE RESORT AREAS IN THE U.S.

5
- TRAVEL TO REGULAR RESORTS IN THE U.S.
- TAKE A CRUISE
- GO SKIING
- BEACH VACATION

4
- FLY TO VACATION RESORTS OCCASIONALLY
- DRIVE TO VACATION SPOTS
- DRIVE TO HOME TOWN ONCE A YEAR

3
- DRIVE TO PARENTS' OR OTHER OUT-OF-TOWN RELATIVES
- A WEEK OF HUNTING OR CAMPING
- STAY HOME OR TAKE A LONG WEEKEND LOCALLY

2
- STAY HOME ON VACATION
- NOT HAVE A VACATION

1
- NO VACATIONS

VACATIONS

MONEY

How Do I Pay for All of This?

Contrary to popular opinion, money is not the most important aspect of the game, nor is the game scored by the amount of wealth one obtains. Rather, the degree to which one becomes fluent in a league's language and makes a contribution in that league becomes the objective and subsequent measurement of success.

Once you are sponsored to a higher position within a level, or reach to a new level altogether, you will be *given* the money necessary to live at that level. Money becomes nothing more than a reward to someone who has been sponsored into a higher level. As an example, you will rarely find anyone getting a promotion without a promotional raise. In any given city, all vice presidents and equivalent positions will pay enough for these players to live in the same neighborhoods and join the same clubs.

When we speak of the wealth that most members of level seven enjoy, we hear it referred to as "Old Money." The label came about because it takes at least one generation before a family usually shows fluency at level seven, and then can be sponsored into that level. The expression "old money can always tell new money," means that "new money" has not learned the fine nuances of the level seven language. It will be up to the children to learn the subtleties of the level and to express them naturally and comfortably. There are many examples in our society where new money has tried to buy its way into the old money group. For example, building the biggest house on the block will not necessarily impress people in Level 7 if other aspects of their culture are not displayed. A light-hearted look at level seven would be the old television program called "The Beverly Hillbillies." The Clampets had the money, but culturally just didn't fit in.

One other note regarding the earnings chart: An individual at a lower level may make more money than someone at a higher level. This is possible since an employee at the lower level may not be promoted because of a lack of fluency at the next level, or simply because the employee doesn't want to be promoted into management. For those individuals who are excellent technical contributors, there are usually many possibilities that allow for additional salary increases. Therefore, it is very possible for a senior sales representative to make more money than a new sales manager. This is an indication that the system does *pay* for performance even though it doesn't necessarily *promote* based on performance.

LEVEL SEVEN

Money for members in this group often has been passed on for many generations, which is why the label frequently applied to this group is "Old Money." Amounts of money may extend beyond millions of dollars.

LEVEL SIX

While this group represents "New Money," the amounts are enormous. The range may be from multi-millions to billions. Many of the richest people in the game play at level six, not at seven.

LEVEL FIVE

Participants may have earnings in the range of $100,000–$500,000 and beyond.

LEVEL FOUR

A range for individuals in this league is $18,000–$250,000. Based on occupation, the range may be even broader.

LEVEL THREE

This level is composed of individuals who are paid by the hour. As a result, the earnings range (through overtime) could surpass levels higher than three. At a minimum, the range may be $12,000–$75,000.

LEVEL TWO

This ranges from $8,000–$35,000 for individuals at this level. This is in connection with part-time employment.

LEVEL ONE

Participants at level one receive government subsidies and/or rely on contributions made by individuals or groups to religious organizations and volunteer agencies.

LEVEL COMPOSITE

L E V E L S

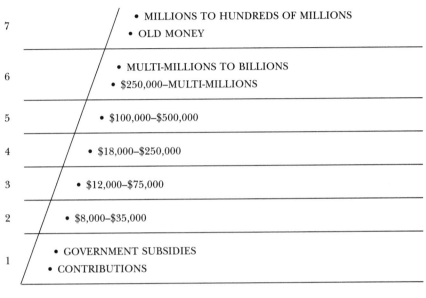

LEVELS	
7	• MILLIONS TO HUNDREDS OF MILLIONS • OLD MONEY
6	• MULTI-MILLIONS TO BILLIONS • $250,000–MULTI-MILLIONS
5	• $100,000–$500,000
4	• $18,000–$250,000
3	• $12,000–$75,000
2	• $8,000–$35,000
1	• GOVERNMENT SUBSIDIES • CONTRIBUTIONS

MONEY

COMMUNITY INVOLVEMENT

For three reasons, this is by far the most important category in the system. First, it allows you to expand your personal network outside of your company. In the days of downsizing and corporate restructuring, no one can be totally assured of a permanent position with an organization. In today's competitive world, boards are even replacing top-level CEO's. Hopefully, this will never happen to you, but if it does, being able to pick up the phone and get your name into "the network" outside of your organization could make a tremendous difference.

Secondly, your organization needs representation at the highest levels in your communities. Whether it's customers who will buy from you in business, volunteers and financial contributors for non-profit organizations, or government budget decision makers for the military or government agencies, no organization can be an island in the system. The number of bridges an organization builds to the community in which they must exist is directly related to the success they will enjoy. Individuals are no exception to this rule. If I am a financial advisor and can comfortably float in top executive circles, I will probably have top executives as a client base.

Thirdly, and most important, this is the essence of what "the game" is all about, *giving something back*. Thank heavens for the Ford and Rockefeller foundations, for through their generosity, poorer folks are educated and cared for. Thank heavens for the United Way volunteers, because the community is made better and safer. Thank heavens for the Boy and Girl Scout volunteers, for our youth will grow up stronger. To be successful in the game and not share that success with the people and communities in which we live might show a narrow perspective about life. If you believe that it is better to give than to receive or that you should treat people as you wish to be treated, then this is the arena to display it. The major difference in new versus old money is simple: New money gets and old money gives. Rarely will you find a multi-billionaire who does not establish channels to give back some of the money before dying. Remember, no one is limited to contributing or "giving back" to any given level. Mother Teresa, for example, didn't have millions of dollars, but has had a pronounced effect upon the world. In President George W. Bush's second State of the Union address, he asked all Americans to volunteer 4,000 hours to their favorite charities.

LEVEL SEVEN

These individuals chair or are on the boards of prominent national non-profit organizations and charities. If not personally active, they will lend their name or financial support to these efforts. The term "philanthropic" will often be applied to the best players at this level.

LEVEL SIX

These individuals take on the same leadership role of players at level seven, but do so on a regional basis. This means serving on the board of the Atlanta United Way or Dallas Symphony verses the National United Way Board or the Board of the New York Philharmonic.

LEVEL FIVE

Level five players will be the top contributors and board members in level five cities (e.g., New Orleans or Richmond) or serve on major committees in major cities such as Chicago and Boston.

LEVEL FOUR

These individuals use their leadership skills to chair committees on non-profit boards and to volunteer for non-profit organizations such as the chamber of commerce and local charities.

LEVEL THREE

Individuals at this level usually volunteer for their immediate community's activities. These include working with the PTA, being a volunteer fireman, coaching a Little League team or acting as a scout leader.

LEVEL TWO

"Giving back" at this level often occurs through the charitable activities of the church or synagogue. It might take the form of a church supper for the homeless or a cake sale.

LEVEL ONE

Individuals at this level are usually not involved in community contributions of time or money. They are usually the recipients of much of the volunteer work done at other levels.

LEVEL COMPOSITE

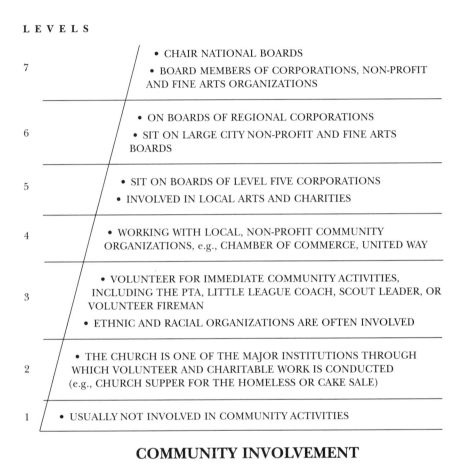

L E V E L S

7
- CHAIR NATIONAL BOARDS
- BOARD MEMBERS OF CORPORATIONS, NON-PROFIT AND FINE ARTS ORGANIZATIONS

6
- ON BOARDS OF REGIONAL CORPORATIONS
- SIT ON LARGE CITY NON-PROFIT AND FINE ARTS BOARDS

5
- SIT ON BOARDS OF LEVEL FIVE CORPORATIONS
- INVOLVED IN LOCAL ARTS AND CHARITIES

4
- WORKING WITH LOCAL, NON-PROFIT COMMUNITY ORGANIZATIONS, e.g., CHAMBER OF COMMERCE, UNITED WAY

3
- VOLUNTEER FOR IMMEDIATE COMMUNITY ACTIVITIES, INCLUDING THE PTA, LITTLE LEAGUE COACH, SCOUT LEADER, OR VOLUNTEER FIREMAN
- ETHNIC AND RACIAL ORGANIZATIONS ARE OFTEN INVOLVED

2
- THE CHURCH IS ONE OF THE MAJOR INSTITUTIONS THROUGH WHICH VOLUNTEER AND CHARITABLE WORK IS CONDUCTED (e.g., CHURCH SUPPER FOR THE HOMELESS OR CAKE SALE)

1
- USUALLY NOT INVOLVED IN COMMUNITY ACTIVITIES

COMMUNITY INVOLVEMENT

LIFESTYLE ACTIVITIES

Categories	One	Two	Three	Four	Five	Six	Seven
Socio-economic Class Titles	Drop-out Class	Next-to-bottom, Welfare, Poverty Class	Labor Class, Lower–Middle, Blue Collar, Working Class	Standard–Middle, Suburban–Middle, White Collar, Professional, Managerial	High Level, Upper Middle Class	Next-to-top, Celebrity, Nouveau Riche, Lower–Upper, Jet Set	Elite, Top, Upper–Upper, Aristocratic, Governing, Old Money
Education	1–2 Years of High School	Possibly High School Degree	Usually High School Degree	Commercial, Associate Degree, Technical and Junior College Degree	College Degree, Solid Schools	Advanced Degree, Better Schools	Advanced Degree, Best Schools, Boarding/Prep Schools
Occupation	Out of Work	Part-time Worker at Minimum Wage	Non-exempt Manual Administrative Workers	Exempt, Accountants, Programmers, Sales Reps, Managers	Middle Management, Small Business Owners, Airline Pilots, Medical Professionals	Regional Politicians, Top Corporate Execs, Movie, T.V., Sports Personalities	Family Business, National Politics, Wall Street Lawyers, Top 20 Banks
Organizations and Clubs	Church Club	Y.M.C.A./Y.W.C.A. Boys/Girls Clubs, Church-Related Clubs	Moose Club, Eagle Lodge, Cultural Clubs, Gun Clubs	Mason, Rotary, Non-profit, Civic Organizations	Neighborhood Country Clubs, Swim/Tennis Clubs	Regional Country Clubs, Local Community and Boards	Exclusive National Social Clubs, Profit & Non-profit National Boards
Social Activities	Church-Related	T.V., Church	Movies, Hunting, Fishing, Camping, Family Activities, Bowling	Entry Level, Theater, Tennis, Golf	More Accomplished in Sports and Cultural Events, Entry Level Skiing & Bridge	Sailing, Skiing, Flying, Charity Drives	Yachting, Horse Breeding, Patron Fine Arts, Fox Hunting, Polo
Location and Type of House	Housing Projects, Inner City, Homeless	Housing Projects, Inner City, Rent Subsidized	Urban Areas, Own Mobile Home, Ethnic Committees	Own Homes in Suburban Communities, Tract Houses	Country Club Communities, In-town Renovations	Extra Large Homes, Custom Built, Tennis Court, Pool	Mansions, Multiple Homes

LIFESTYLE ACTIVITIES (continued)

Categories	One	Two	Three	Four	Five	Six	Seven
Entertaining in the Home	Rarely Entertain	Extended Family Members, Holidays	Family & Friends, Barbecues, Casual	Social Cocktail Parties, Self Prepared, Sporty	Cocktail Parties, Business & Social, Catered, Dressy	Dinner Parties Business & Social, Catered, Dressy	Dinner Parties, Very Political, Extravagant, Formal
Earning Power	None	$8,000–$35,000	$12,000–$75,000	$18,000–$250,000	$100,000–$500,000	$250,000–Millions and above	Millions, Inherited Wealth
Other Investments	None	None	Savings Series "E" Bonds, Lottery Tickets	Inner City Condo IRAs, C.D.s, Treasury Bonds	Vacation Home, Investment Portfolio	Limited/General Partnership, Revenue Producing Properties	Stock Ownership, Interlocking Directories
Fine Arts	Never Attend Theater	Rarely Attend Theater	Attend Popular Theater Productions	Mainly Theater, Some Ballet, Opera, Symphony, Museum	Season Tickets, Ballet, Opera, Symphony, Museum	Serve on Fine Arts Committees & Boards	Patron of the Fine Arts
Car	No Car	1 Used Car	Intermediate Used, Pick-up Truck	Big American Car, 1 Other Used Car	Mercedes, Cadillac, Other Luxury Cars	Rolls Royce, Bentley, Multiple Cars	Chauffeur Driven Limousine
Vacation Activities	None	Home to Parents	1 Week Family Vacation, Home to Parents	1 Week Shore, Mountains, 1 Week, Home to Parents	U.S.A. Vacation, Cruises, Shore, Mountains	Exclusive Resorts Abroad Once a Year	Most Exclusive Resorts, Extended Vacation Abroad, Seasonal Homes
Committees & Boards	Not Involved	Involved in Church Work	Non-Profit Volunteer Work in Ethnic Community	On Committees of Mainstream Non-Profit Organizations	Chair Committees of Major Non-Profit Organizations	On Boards: Non-Profit Regional Corporation, Local Arts	Chair Boards of National Non-Profit Major Corp., Fine Arts

The grid on the previous two pages combines the pyramids we have discussed along with a few additional ones. Once they are put together, they form a language or culture. With the grids, you should be able to determine the level into which you were born, the level to which you might have moved, and what level to which you might want to advance. Remember, once a person becomes comfortable or fluent in the level above, someone will sponsor that person to that next level. Once sponsored, it is the obligation of that sponsor to ensure you have the financial means to stay there.

It is also important to remember that this is just a model for consideration—only *you*, through your observations and experiences, can define the game board for your career. Your honest and accurate assessments are the only things that will allow you to make the right choices for your life. But please always remember, just because you don't like the rules or wish they would change doesn't eliminate the reality of what the rules are.

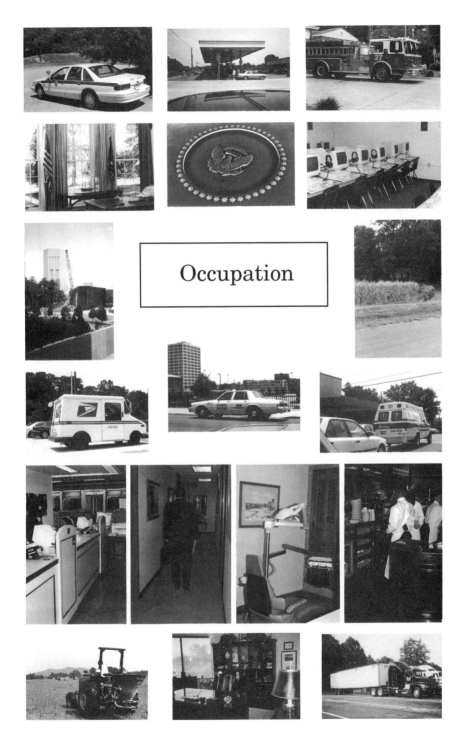

Occupation

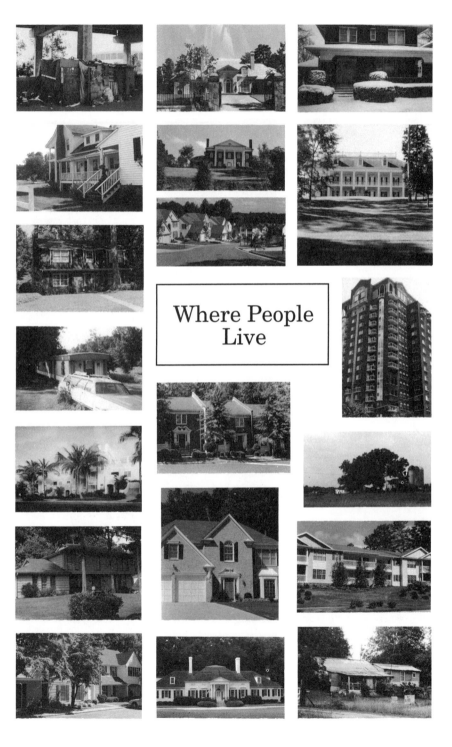

Where People
Live

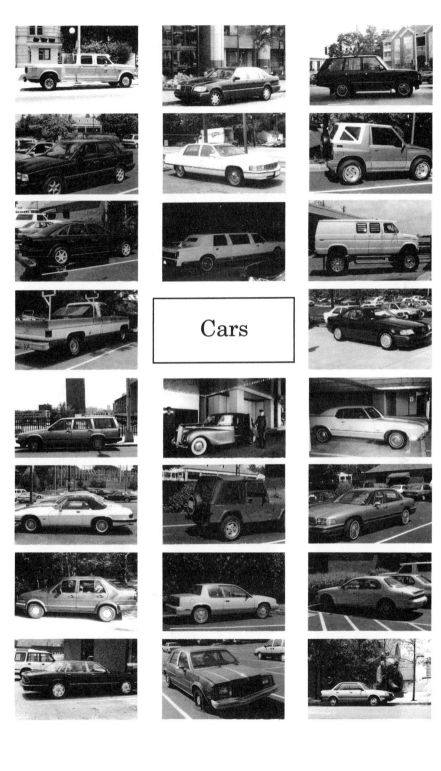

Cars

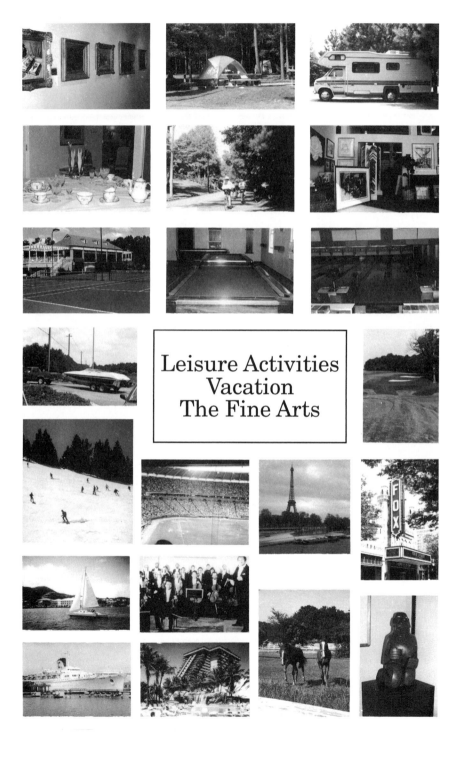

Leisure Activities
Vacation
The Fine Arts

Summary of the Rules

Now that we have seen the game board, we are able to understand that our societal culture is not just one language, rather, it is composed of seven different languages. This information will help us better understand the intricacies of the corporate game. We have also seen that these languages affect all other disciplines including politics, government, military, education, religion, science, non-profit, science/engineering, and society as a whole.

To master the system, you must find where you want to make a contribution, develop the language of the level you want, then become fluent in that language. At that point, a sponsor will recognize your fluency and pull you into the higher level. Once you have been sponsored into a level, it is the obligation of your sponsor and other members of that level to ensure that you have enough money to remain there. Remember, you cannot buy your way into the next level. Anyone who goes only after money will not successfully advance through the structure. You *must* be sponsored.

Here is a summary of the unwritten rules that have been suggested in this chapter:

1. ***Every Person Is Born into a Class Level***
   This is the lifestyle achieved by your parents at the time of your birth.

2. ***Jobs and Positions in Organizations Correspond to Socio-Economic Class* Levels**
   Each job, from entry level to executive management, will fit into the level structure.

3. *Money Is Not the Sole Criterion of Level Acceptance*
You can't buy class, a promotion, or the ability to execute a given language at another level. You must pay your dues! These dues come in the form of learning to be comfortable in the lifestyle of the level to which you want to advance.

4. *An Individual Must Be Sponsored into the Next Level*
People do things for others with whom they are comfortable. It is necessary for an individual to demonstrate the capability of functioning at a higher job level to get a sponsor. Prior to achieving the level, an individual must act and look the part before getting the part.

5. *Levels Are Possessive of Their Members*
Once a comfort level is established, individuals do not want to lose members of their group (this includes friends, neighbors, work associates, and even family). Comments of disapproval are often heard when the lifestyle activities of a higher group are displayed by individual.

6. *Once Entrance to a Level Is Gained, the Financial Support for You to Stay Will Be* **Provided**
When you see raises given in organizations, contracts awarded to businesses, and financial deals shared with friends, you are seeing the results of an act of sponsorship. Whether directly or indirectly given, providing money is the obligation of any sponsor.

7. *People Do Not Necessarily Want a Title . . .*
   They Want a Lifestyle
   Although titles are important and valued, the ability to live a specific lifestyle tends to be more important. The president of a small company and the president of a Fortune Top 20 company carry the same title, but will live completely different lifestyles.

8. *Whoever Is at the Top of a Pyramid Has the Right*
   to Make the Rules
   Systems and organizations must have rules to prevent chaos and anarchy. The dynamics of the system indicates power flows downward. This leaves the ultimate responsibility for setting a direction dictating the rules to the individual at the top.

9. *When You're Through Changing, You Are Through*
   Change is a fact of life. Self-improvement and personal growth have long been associated with success. When people choose to halt their growth, they have also made a choice to halt their advancement in the game.

10. **Execution** *Is the Name of the Game*
    Understanding what is required is not enough. An individual, to be effective, must use all acquired skills and knowledge to make it happen.

These ten rules sound fairly simple and straightforward. So do the rules of golf. But how many of us can play eighteen holes within the regulation number of strokes? The *execution* of the rules will eventually decide the winners in any game, be it golf or business.

"Birds of a feather will flock together."

"You are who you hang out with."

"We are all born into a lifestyle."

"Money is the result of sponsorship;
sponsorship is a result of lifestyle."

"You must look and act the part,
before you can get the part."

"People will not sponsor anyone into their
group until they are sure the person can
comfortably execute the rules."

"Money is not the sole criterion of class
acceptance."

CHAPTER 7

Game Skills

Now that you better understand the game board and how you can move from one level to the next, you are only limited by your ability and willingness to execute. You must first make a decision on whether you want to be a vertical or horizontal player. Once this is done, there are some useful skills which will help you to become more effective in reaching your specific objectives. The most critical skills to master are *goal setting, emotional control, delegation,* and *planning*. These just happen to be the most difficult as well. Let's take a more detailed look at each one.

Goal Setting

Since every choice we make on the game board moves us in a specific direction, it is important to know where we want to go. When Alice asked the Cheshire Cat how to get out of Wonderland, his wise reply was, "It all depends on where you want to go!" If you don't know where you are going, any road will get you there.

Setting goals is essential for a serious game player. In order to stay motivated and successful in the game, you must decide: *What do I want out of life? What do I wish to leave behind as my legacy? What will make me feel successful? What will make me happy?* On a higher philosophical note, answers to such questions might also help resolve additional puzzles like: *Who am I? Why am I here? What is life really all about?* All of these questions are important and have held the attention of many great philosophers and theologians for centuries. Although important, be careful that these issues and concerns don't bog you down to the point of immobility. Hopefully, as we move through life and deal with the lesser issues, the greater ones will also be resolved.

Where should we start in the goal-setting process? The first step is to simply choose the lifestyle you want. If, at retirement, you feel you would be comfortable at a level four occupation and lifestyle, then target your efforts to that end. If you want to be at level six, then begin your preparation for that level. However, it is necessary to be realistic about the trade-offs you are willing to make to achieve a specific level.

Goal setting isn't a once-in-a-lifetime experience! You might start out wanting level three, but after you get there, you realize that level four or five is more desireable, and also more realistic. "The game" requires a continual growth process and it is a good idea to periodically review your goals and adjust or change them when necessary.

A major oversight in the goal-setting process is to forget that "the game" involves more than just your commitment. It is a couples game. It is possible for two individuals to choose very different lifestyle objectives and wind up playing in two different leagues, which, of course, causes friction at home. When this happens, couples become liabilities to one another instead of assets. Therefore, it is extremely important for couples to review life objectives as a team, identify where and how they need to compromise, and then settle on joint goals, many of which may be temporary.

If both partners agree on their ultimate objective, they will be able to begin preparing their fluency in the targeted language very early in their lives. Then, as they progress up the pyramid to the more advanced levels, they will gain a better perspective of the upper level requirements and decide if they really want to advance further or if the trade-offs are just too much. However, both must agree on the trade-offs to make the partnership workable.

Setting goals seems like an easy process, but it can be very difficult. Many people in their thirties and even forties often say, "I still don't know what I want to do or be when I grow up!" To simplify the process, divide your goals into *long-term, mid-term,* and *immediate* categories. Once long-term lifestyle objectives have been set, you can more easily assess whether the immediate goals (six months to two years) are ones that will lead to your mid- and long-term objectives.

Tips for Setting Goals

If you are going through a period of confusion in your life, don't panic. You might want to step out of your busy daily routine to do some reflecting. This may be the perfect time for that vacation to take you away from it all for a while. Remember, very few people escape these doubting periods, so you are not alone. If we are lucky, we might have a long life and enough time to get it all done, if we just keep moving ahead!

- Allow family and friends to help you through conversations about your plans, as well as getting their opinions. Although you have to make the ultimate decision about your life, hearing opinions of others you trust may help clear the log jams.

- Try putting yourself into new environments and situations to test if you like them. Trying some new lifestyle activities could open the door to different worlds or show you that those worlds are not as much fun as the one in which you are currently operating.

- Lastly, don't put so much energy into achieving your goals that you forget to have fun where you are now. Remember, life is not a destination—it is a journey; it is learning from and enjoying all the experiences along the way!

Emotional Control

Much like any other contest or sporting event, "the game" can be emotional. However, the moment you allow emotions to drive your decisions, you are in trouble. Decisions made under stress and emotion are sometimes regretted later. Although it is difficult, we must rise above day-to-day combat, release ourselves from the emotion, and take an overall look at the game board. Only then can we make decisions that will be lasting and successful. For example, quitting your job because you had a bad week or leaving your industry because you don't get along with your boss may be emotional decisions that you will regret later. The ability to rise above immediate emotions to view long-term solutions is truly a talent.

Losing control might not only affect our ability to make sound decisions and/or to set realistic goals, but can also have a negative impact on our important relationships. People who cannot or do not control their emotions have a tendency to strike out at other people, causing disruptions and even pain to others. In these emotional states, negative chips are passed on to others. The cutting comments or aggressive non-verbal gestures might be overlooked by a family member or the significant other in your life (at least for a while), but a potential sponsor does not usually have the time or patience to put up with such behavior. Why should they? There are many capable competitors who do not leave people "bleeding" after an interaction, and they are far less risky to sponsor!

If statements such as, "He's always flying off the handle," or "She lets people get under her skin," have ever been applied to you, this is an indication that you need to work on this area. Sponsors may interpret these actions as your inability to handle pressure or to think clearly in a crisis. Either way, it could spell doom to future career advancement.

Solutions to Controlling Emotions

Get control of your hot buttons. We all have them, and the people who are close to us know them very well. If they find themselves in a competitive situation with us, they will push those buttons and render us ineffective. This is very much like a sports competitor who gets into the "heads" of his opponents. Our family members, social acquaintances, and working associates do the very same thing. The solution is to not let them push the buttons. If you let them, *they control you.* In essence, whenever they pull your strings, you dance! The best reaction in these situations is no reaction. Take time to let your emotions settle. Take a deep breath, count to ten, walk away, and collect yourself before you speak. We have heard these rules all our lives, and they *do* work! However, if you have strong emotional tendencies, you know these rules are not always easy to follow.

For long-term decisions, there is often enough time to calm down before giving a response. However, the immediate flare-ups can be extremely harmful. Sometimes, a negative look or a certain tone of voice is all that is necessary to do major damage to a relationship. Constantly apologizing for emotional reactions wears thin very quickly. Here are some guidelines to help control your emotions:

- Remember that although you always have the right to express your opinions, you also have an obligation to leave people "whole." Your opinions should be shared for the purpose of influencing others, not to put them down or hurt them. It is possible, with practice, to let people know that you respect them and their feelings, even though you disagree with what they are saying. A spoonful of sugar will always help any medicine go down.

- Be open to other opinions. We like to be right, but the truth is, we cannot be right all the time! When we are not, more than likely someone is trying to give us the right answer. If we control our emotions, we will be able to hear that answer.

- Be an active listener; don't just react to information. Ask questions that will give you more knowledge about the situation and listen to the response. Don't assume the answer.

- Don't take everything personally. Of course, we are all important, but I doubt that any rule in this world-wide system was put into place with you or me specifically in mind! If we can see the bigger picture rather than just the detail, it helps us to control our emotions. One of my favorite thoughts is that we should always soar with the eagles—fly above it all.

In response to the question, "Do *I* have to do it?," look around and observe the exceptions, if any, to the rules. At each level there are rewarded behaviors, but when our behavior is not acceptable, generally we are not rewarded by others at that level; we are simply tolerated for a while. Remember, "As long as you live (or work) under my roof. . . ." The people at the top of the pyramid have the right to make the rules and also to expect others to follow them.

Delegation

One of the essential elements in this game is time. We must create time to plan and to execute our decisions. That is why the skill of delegation is critical. Many believe this skill is easy to learn, thinking that, "If all I have to do is to give my work away, I can learn this skill quickly!" Not necessarily. You see, delegation is a frame of mind, and if you come from a background of "doers," or if growing up you heard the expression, "If you want something done right, do it yourself," if you ever say to yourself, "No one can do it better than me," or "This is a job I must handle," then you could have a hard time with delegation.

Before we get too far into a discussion on delegation, it is important to remind ourselves that delegation does not mean abandoning personal responsibilities or a reduction in quality. Dedication to getting the work completed in a quality manner is still necessary. The result will simply be less time-consuming for you than doing all of the work yourself.

Gaining more time for ourselves may be easier than we might first have imagined. Consider paying a neighborhood teenager to cut your lawn so you will be able to play a round of golf. This might help your golf game, allow you to relax, and may give you some good exposure; it also benefits the person who accepts the delegated task. As a result, we are no longer a prisoner to the detail that can suffocate us. If you become bogged down in the day-to-day details, valuable time that could be used for planning ahead will be lost.

By the time individuals enter into level six, they have mastered delegation, as they delegate almost everything. Lawn, housecleaning, cooking, and babysitting can all be delegated to someone else for a fee. At this point you might be thinking, "If I had their money, I would delegate everything, too!" The key, though, is that these individuals learn to delegate *before* they get to level six. The sooner one learns to delegate, the sooner one can take planning and strategic control of "the game." If you are waiting to delegate when you reach level six, you will probably never reach that level.

Just as the neighborhood teenager benefits from your playing golf and not cutting the grass, delegation at work is one of the best people development tools managers have at their disposal. People grow mainly because of their ability to try new experiences, to do things they have never done before, and even by being allowed to make mistakes and to learn from them.

Usually, the manager who hordes all the difficult assignments also hordes the presentations and exposure to upper management. That manager will not be a popular one with his or her people. They will see their manager as a person unwilling to share either the glory or the exposure that would help the players on the team. President Reagan had a sign on the corner of his desk in the Oval Office that read, "You can accomplish anything you want, as long as you don't care who gets the credit." This is the attitude of an effective executive.

Many administrative assistants find it no challenge or fun to type letters that have been written by others, for this relegates them to being nothing more than a machine. A positive act of delegation would be to encourage your secretary, who normally knows the company functions and individuals associated with those functions, to route letters of request or draft letters of response for your final approval. Oh, I know what you might be saying—"Nobody can write letters like I do." Well, please get over it. This simple act of trust gives individuals an active role in improving your time management, helping paper flow, and gives them an opportunity to show their creativity. By the way, don't forget to give them the credit. Anyone who does this, and who holds a position of responsibility, has just made an ally. And since this game is all about people, an ally is a cherished asset.

Delegation Suggestions

- Eliminate the excuses that prevent delegation. We all have them and always think ours are valid. If you always feel that only you can do a certain job, think about what your organization would do if you never showed up again. Would they go under? Of course not. After a short period of adjustment, your organization would survive and go on. However, by delegating areas of your expertise, the organization grows another level of expertise and you are freed up for potential future movement.

- Review activities, both at home and at work, to see where delegation may be appropriate. At home, consider using outside services and family members. Many experts suggest that one-half of everything we do can be successfully delegated.

- Remember, don't abdicate responsibility for the task after you have delegated it. You must ensure that it is completed to your standards, no matter who helps you, and hold them accountable. This is why giving credit away does not hurt. Everyone already knows who is responsible.

- Use delegation as a development tool. When you delegate an important task to an inexperienced employee, don't abandon the novice. Use this opportunity to teach and make people confident. Naturally, the more you delegate, the better your people will become. Eventually, they will be able to take over.

- Do not feel threatened by other people's successes. If you are doing a good job at delegation, other people will succeed. Try not to compete with them. There is a major dividing line between "expert and doer" versus "leader and executive." Those who cannot make the transition cannot move to higher levels.

- Use time gained from delegation wisely. Resentment grows in those who receive your delegated tasks when you do not make positive use of your newly found time. Playing golf may be a good use of your time instead of cutting grass, but your employees might not appreciate it as much. Keep them informed as to what you have accomplished because of their efforts.

Planning

Once you have set goals for yourself, you are now confronted with the challenge of reaching them. This is where the skill of planning can help you get through the obstacles which may get in your way. To work effectively, good planing requires both knowledge of the situation and creative problem solving. Can you reach objectives without a plan? Yes. However, the risk of not getting there or being delayed goes up dramatically! Whenever your objective is competitive and other competent players have equal skills and a plan, they tend to get there first. Can you imagine top level athletic teams going into competition without a game plan? This would be unthinkable if they really wanted to win!

Planning is an activity that helps you keep score on how well you are doing. Once your objective has been set, the major task of planning is to anticipate all of those things that might happen to keep you from reaching your goal. The positive thing about this process is that you can plan solutions to those obstacles *before* you begin. The challenge is to be able to recognize the potential obstacles. Your ability to anticipate all of them helps to make your plan solid and ensures your success.

As an example, you are going to your manager to ask for two more people for your department. You know that there is a freeze on head count. You have anticipated that your manager will also object because your department got the last two new hires. So, if two more people are brought aboard, your peer manager will have first choice. Tough obstacles to overcome, right?

However, if you have planned well, you will have a response to these objections. You will have weighed the work load and can justify the fact that the two should come to you. But what if during the meeting your manager also says that:

—your new projects are of short duration for such high long-term overhead;

—there is no available office space for any new hires;

—you should complete some of the older projects before starting newer ones;

—if you receive two more people it will create a morale problem with the other managers.

In this case, your planning skills were successful in identifying and resolving two concerns but not enough to get you two new people! When you are able to hit six out of six or seven out of seven, batting 1,000 not only with the objections but winning with solutions, then you will be able to reach the objectives you have set for yourself.

Suggestions for Planning

When preparing a request that will be directed to your boss, a peer, an employee, a spouse, a friend, or to one of your children, the following checklist will allow you to effectively plan.

1. *What is my objective?* Whether it is for a meeting, a request from a family member or friend, or for your career objectives, knowing what you want becomes crucial to success.

2. *What will be the benefit to the individual to whom I am making the request?* This is one of the most important aspects of planning, for, yet again, the game is about people. When we fail to explain the benefits that the person will realize by granting our request, we put the request in jeopardy. In essence, we must crawl into the head of the person to whom we are making the request and see it from their perspective. If they can see no benefit, why should they honor your request?

Employee A will request a project and a raise this way: "Boss, I've been here for ten years. I've worked for you for four years. I've worked awfully hard, and I have done a very good job. I think I deserve a raise." Sorry! The only benefit the boss hears is one directed to the employee. Executives haven't earned their positions by giving away the company's money every time someone gains enough courage to request a raise. In addition, the above request is riddled with self directed "I" statements.

Employee B approaches the situation differently: "Boss, I've worked for the company for ten years. I've worked for you for four of those ten, and during those four years I have gotten to know every department head in the plant. I have established an excellent rapport with the section chiefs. The project coming up next is one that requires someone with these kinds of skills. I know that if assigned, I will be able to return to you at least a twenty-five percent increase in productivity, simply because of my ability to coordinate with the departments. If I understand your compensation plan, that will give you an additional $10,000 in personal bonuses this year." Employee B is on the right track and will most likely get the project and his raise.

3. *What obstacles will keep me from getting my request or stop me from reaching my goals?* Again, your ability to think of as many obstacles as possible will determine the effectiveness of your plan.

4. *What response or action steps will overcome the obstacles identified in the preceding question?* This is the step in the process when a player can begin to use all of his/her experience, uniqueness, and creative problem-solving abilities. This is where individual talent will show. If you can come up with new, innovative approaches beyond those of your competitors, then you should carry the day.

5. *What alternatives may I suggest that I can live with if I don't get my initial request or reach my original goal?* This is not a perfect world, and the best laid plans often go astray! Be prepared for the worst. You can, however, salvage something if you have thought of alternative solutions before you go into battle. By having a compromising position, you are still in control of your desired direction. For example, after an in-depth discussion in the case of the manager requesting two new hires, it might be a relief for the boss to settle on one new hire. If this is something the person bringing the request can live with, then at least a partial victory has been won.

You can see by these action steps that planning does not come easily. A lot of time and attention must be given to do it right. That is why not getting bogged in the details becomes so important. It is very difficult to fight our daily challenges, control our emotions in times of difficulty and stress and still have time for strategic thinking. However, if we can master these two factors, we will be able to avoid the land mines that keep us from reaching our objectives.

Power—The Ability to Influence

Power is often viewed negatively because of how it is used. In reality, power is simply "the ability to influence a person or situation." There are several ways an individual may gain influence.

Position Power

One of the primary ways is to seek a higher position. This is one of the reasons why so many people define success as upward growth. We know in an organization that a president has more influence than a vice president; a general more than a colonel; a bishop more than a minister or priest.

We all have seen situations where someone of a lesser rank might have more influence over the organization than his or her superior, but that is because of other power-based reasons, not position power. Position power only gives you the right to be influential. However, if you do not use this right, over time, you will lose that power base. In organizations, these people are known as weak managers. Let's take, for example, a manager who announces that he or she wants all staff members to report to work at 8:00 a.m. One of the staff members continually comes in between 8:30 and 9:00 a.m. Others will observe what the manager does to this individual. If there are no negative repercussions, it won't take long before the rest of the staff start reporting in on their own time schedules. Eventually, the manager's influence will be watered down in other areas as well. Power not used will evaporate over time.

Knowledge Is Power

We have heard this all of our lives, and it is valid. Knowing what you are doing, and what you need to do, allows you to do a better job. We all are aware that a person who does not know his discipline cannot be an excellent performer. However, a word of caution is necessary if you choose to gain all of your influence in this manner.

Although knowledge can give a short-term boost to your power rating, it normally is limited in scope and short-lived in duration. This type of power fades quickly, once others learn more than you, when the state of the art changes on you (as it does quickly these days), or when you go through a period of performance failures. People have short memories, and the hero one year may become the scapegoat the next.

As a result of this short-term power status, many people who only use this means will not share their knowledge with others for fear of losing their power. You can easily see how this could have a negative effect on a team when the senior engineer only gives the new trainee half an answer! In order to maintain power through knowledge, you must constantly update your skills and then apply them to a good performance effort.

Charismatic Power

Charisma is difficult to define. Some believe it is the vibrations a person gives off, others believe it is the way one carries oneself. We have seen in our presidential campaigns that the charismatic candidate is usually the ultimate winner. The Kennedy-Nixon debates is one of the classic examples of this concept. It is generally conceded that Nixon won the debates, but Kennedy had the charisma and ultimately prevailed. We all might have witnessed a striking woman who walks into a ballroom with a long flowing gown and everyone stops and stares at her. She has just captured the room with charismatic power.

Charisma is often used to separate the many hard workers in the organization and to make the final selection as to who is placed on the high potential list. Remember, we are paid for our performance, but we are promoted based on someone's assessment of our potential. Much of this is based on the charisma or image we project.

Power by Association

People who are close to power often carry the mantle of that power. You have seen administrative assistants or secretaries to the president who are more powerful than vice presidents in the organization. The chairman's son starts his career in the mail room, but few are surprised that he ends up in an executive position. Associating with the power group can do a variety of things for your career. First, it allows you the opportunity to better learn the value systems, the actions, and activities of the executive culture. Since knowledge is power, this knowledge is essential to your ultimate acceptance by members in that group. Second, people outside the group will view you as a person who might be "wired." As a result, they will treat you a little differently and listen to your suggestions more intently. Third, being in the power network allows the executive group to teach you about their world and to decide if they want you to become part of their group. We have already concluded that no one moves through the system without a sponsor.

Does Any of This Sound Familiar?

Does this discussion about power sound familiar? It clearly should! All one has to do is change some of the terms—knowledge (doing a good job), charisma (viewed by others) and association (visibility and reputation)—to Performance, Image, and Exposure, and we have come full circle with our P.I.E. discussion. It's true! P.I.E. (Performance, Image, and Exposure) is nothing more than how one can get more influence in the organization and the general community. An effective Performance, Image, and Exposure plan is nothing more than a good power plan.

Using Power

Once you have passed the minimum acceptable standards required of Performance, Image, and Exposure, you must then go forth looking for opportunities to apply your new-found influence. The best opportunity to use power is to address problems in the organization that are not being resolved. Power players are constantly asking themselves, "How can we do this better?" It is only when power is sought for the selfish gain of the individual (building an empire for oneself) that we view power as negative. If a person wants a management job only because it will provide him or her with a corner office, special parking privileges, and a membership to a club, then he wants the job only for the personal power it carries. Very quickly he will be labeled as "all style and no substance."

But if you want the job because there is a major flaw in the marketing organization's communication link to the sales force, and you can fix it, then you're seeking the promotion in a positive manner. Your abilities could bring hundreds of thousands of dollars of additional revenue to the organization. You are a team player, desiring the power for the good of the organization. Incidentally, those who pursue power out of a positive motivation frequently move up faster than the other type of manager and will still get the corner office and other perks, even though it was not their intent.

Positive power adds dynamic energy to an organization, since the focus is on team success instead of individual success. Of course, individual success is virtually assured when the team wins. When managers and employees look for ways to work more effectively, for ways to test new theories, or when they are taking risks in order to help the organization run smoothly, then the entire work atmosphere changes. Power players are constantly on the watch for individuals who complain that "It's not my job!" To the power player, that statement spells opportunity. Something isn't getting done. Once you identify an opportunity, use the skills we have discussed, which include risk-taking, planning, goal setting, and problem solving. If used effectively, you can assume promotions and greater influence will follow.

How to Keep Power

If power comes down to doing positive things for the organization, it makes sense to assume that you need good, loyal people around you to keep your power. Once again, it boils down to people. There are several things that can be done to maintain your power base of good people.

—*Treat people with respect.* Show them that they are important to you. In those times when your budget won't allow you to hand out expensive rewards, a simple "Thank you" will go a long way.

—*See people as individuals.* Everyone is unique and would like to be so considered. The outgrowth of this may have positive and powerful ramifications. By recognizing and developing people's uniqueness, you will always have a source of new ideas and different approaches from which to choose when problem solving is necessary.

—*Delegate meaningful tasks to people.* Although small tasks must be delegated as well, the challenging jobs are the ones that get people fired up. These are the tasks they can get their teeth into and will help them with their personal growth. Managers who grow their people are the managers who can maintain employee loyalty.

—*Empower your people.* When handing out assignments, there is a tendency to hand out the answer as well. After all, you're the boss! However, this reduces the assignment to busy work. Allow people to own the assignment and let them make it theirs. Depending on how new they are to the organization, you must offer guidance from afar. This will strengthen loyalty and grow people at the same time.

—*Listen to what they have to say.* One of the greatest compliments we can give people is to stop everything we are doing and listen. This says they are important and what they have to say is important, as well. You don't have to agree with everything a person says, but by listening you can better explain your points of disagreement. On the other hand, they, at least, had a chance to speak their mind and be heard.

—*Be open and honest.* Level with people. Most people want to know where they stand with their boss. To do otherwise is to create mistrust, which will eventually dissolve your power base. How many times have we heard an employee say, "I have a tough, demanding manager, but you know one thing about her, she's fair." Not a bad comment for any manager to hear from an employee.

—*Be flexible.* We can't be right all of the time! During those moments when we realize that our point of view is not the best, change it. Phrases like, "You were right on this one," or "I was off base, let's change strategy," are powerful in building team loyalty and a strong power base.

—*Be a mentor for your people.* Everyone could use help. Offer ideas, suggestions, and feedback to your employees. While these are not often comfortable skills to execute, they contain the messages that will encourage employee growth and development.

Goal Setting

"If you don't know where you are going, you might end up someplace else."

Emotional Control

"Count to ten before you speak."

"Always look before you leap."

Delegation

"Don't get bogged down in the detail of life."

"You can accomplish anything you want as long as you don't care who gets the credit."

Ronald Reagan

Planning

"The best laid plans often go astray."

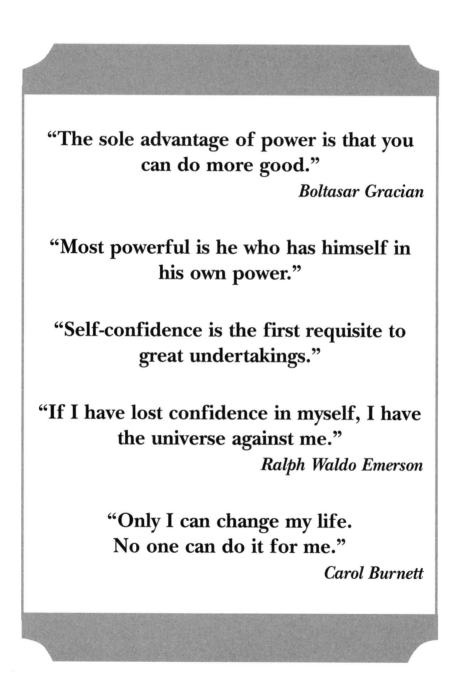

"The sole advantage of power is that you can do more good."

Boltasar Gracian

"Most powerful is he who has himself in his own power."

"Self-confidence is the first requisite to great undertakings."

"If I have lost confidence in myself, I have the universe against me."

Ralph Waldo Emerson

"Only I can change my life. No one can do it for me."

Carol Burnett

CHAPTER 8

Why Are the Rules Important?

Hopefully, by now you might agree that there is a system to any and every society that constitutes the "rules of the game." Without this system there would be chaos, disorder, and even anarchy. But the question might still remain as to "how do I put this information to use in my life?" The core benefit comes from the age-old adage that you cannot play a game unless you know the rules of that game. The same is true in the game of life. If anyone wants to be empowered, take control, be their own person, a person must know the rules by which the game is played. These decisions start at the very beginning of life's decision-making process. They might include: Should I stay in school? What courses should I take? What campus social activities should I be involved in? Decisions later in life will include what neighborhood to live in, clothes to wear, and activities for your children.

Life is truly a game of choices, and it is essential, if you are to be empowered, that everyone knows the choices they need to make, as well as the short- and long-term ramifications of those choices. The decision to drop out of high school will have a definite impact on that young person for the rest of their life. This does not mean that the choice cannot be changed twenty or thirty years later. All a person needs to do is make the choice of obtaining their General Education Degree (G.E.D.), and then more of life's choices will open up to them. The great thing about the game of life we are playing is that it is never too late. As Yogi Berra, manager of the New York Yankees, once said, "It ain't over till it's over."

Career Planning

Some of the critical choices we all make are the ones involving our careers. This starts at the junior high school level when deciding to take a trade preparedness curriculum instead of courses in math and science and continues on to the work environment when one chooses to become a manager or to remain a non-exempt employee.

A major factor often overlooked in preparing for future positions is when individuals concentrate on developing the technical skills needed for future employment (such as accounting and engineering skills) but will often neglect the language (lifestyle skills) that must be spoken at that higher level. Remember, no matter how technically efficient you might be at that higher job, if it requires a level change, no one can sponsor you until you fluently speak the language of that upper level.

The higher you rise on the game board, the more social involvement is required of your position. This might mean holding or attending cocktail functions for your organization as well as attending banquets or charity functions. However, having a "significant other" at the mid-level and a spouse at upper level functions becomes significant. For this reason, joint career planning with your mate is essential. If one of the individuals in the couple is not aware or willing to support these activities, then your ability to compete will be reduced substantially. At the upper levels, career planning really becomes life or lifestyle planning with couples agreeing on events to be attended, new skills to be learned, and the amount of commitment to be made in pursuit of upper level objectives.

Mentoring Others

Mentoring is the act of helping others grow in order for them to reach their potential and achieve their goals. The game is riddled with so many land mines and unknown pitfalls it is virtually impossible to maneuver through and around the organizational ladder without a mentor. It is the duty of any mentor to be available to help their mentee with current challenges, give feedback when warranted, and, most importantly, prepare their mentee for future responsibility.

One of the major omissions of many mentors is they concentrate on giving advise in the technical arena and not prepare mentees for the lifestyle requirements of future executive positions. Understanding the rules of the game and all of its requirements allow both mentor and mentee to not only visually see the future position desired by the mentee but to also identify the social skills that the future positions will require. When discussing these requirements on a level-by-level basis, it tends to make these requirements more generic and less personal. These discussions become less of identifying inadequacies of the mentee and more the simple identification of the requirements all players must consider for future advancement.

Sometimes people are very threatened with the challenge of learning new skills, new activities, and being forced into new lifestyle experiences. They often throw out the resistance statements of "I want to be myself" or even "If I did those new things, I would feel like I was selling myself out." Those statements are often the basis of being afraid of the unknown, becoming too comfortable with current life situations, or even fear of possible failure if they try something new. At a minimum, those statements might suggest that if they try something new they will look foolish to people who are already comfortable with the lifestyle activities you are suggesting they try. The fact is, everyone must pay his or her dues in this game. The rules go on to suggest "you pay me now or you pay me later, but everyone must eventually pay their dues." For example, the chairman's son might have grown up in a country club environment and educated in private school. This means usually that the chairman's son has learned how to play golf, tennis, ski, sail, and understand fine arts. It is an indicator that the chairman's son has had exposure to the upper level language at an early age and thus has become familiar and comfortable with these activities early in life. He has paid his dues. It, however, does not negate the responsibility of someone not exposed to these activities early in life to become involved and knowledgeable at a later time in life. The dues must be paid.

One of the responses I have found helpful to the statement "I want to be me" is to ask the individual to think back twenty years and recall the dress code they had, the activities in which they participated, and the lifestyle they lived. Once they described themselves twenty years ago, the question you should ask next is "Were you yourself twenty years ago?" Of course, the answer is always "Yes." The next question is "Have you changed your dress, activities, and lifestyle in the last twenty years?" More than likely you will get the response "Yes." Your next question will comfortably fall into perspective: "If you were a different *you* twenty years ago, and you are still *you* today, why can't we imagine that you will be still a *different you* twenty years from now?" The point being of course, anyone defining him or herself strictly at one point in their life and never changes that perspective has and/or will stop all self-growth and self-improvement. We will always be changing, but we will always be ourselves. Remember, "When you're through changing, you are through."

Mentoring Our Children

One of the most important responsibilities of any parent or grandparent is to be a mentor to their children. It is a natural instinct to want your children to climb on your shoulders and achieve the life goals you (the parent/grandparent) wished for yourself but were unable to attain. That is why parents without college educations insist their children attend college or even if they do not like the ballet ensure their children enroll in a dance class. Understanding the rules allow parents to make lifestyle exposure decisions for their children.

If I might share a personal example: As young parents my wife and I had numerous discussions about whether we should enroll our children in private school. She insisted we should; however, my position was clear. At the time, our children were already attending one of the better public schools in the state, and I felt since I was a public school graduate and turned out fairly well balanced, I concluded public school was the way to go. Public school would keep their feet on the ground—keep them in touch with people. After all, if it was good enough for me, it should be good enough for them.

Unfortunately, once I learned the advantages of attending a private school, my children were firmly entrenched in their public school life and had no desire to leave their friends and public school activities for uncharted waters. For me to insist, I realized the upheaval could cause major damage. With my newfound understanding of the game, one day I sat down to analyze what my children might be missing in their future by not attending private school. One of the areas in which I felt they needed more exposure was the fine arts. The compromise I made with them was that they could stay in public school as long as they compensated by attending fine art events or watching approved programs broadcasted on public television. These events would also be tied to their monthly allowances. With the prospect of not having to leave their friends, they quickly agreed, and the new system was put into place.

The first test of this system came when my second child, at the age of twelve, was asked to attend a performance of the ballet. My wife and I had purchased season tickets, and I remember calling him away from the neighborhood baseball game to get dressed for his first ballet experience. I was harangued by comments like "Why do I have to do this, none of my friends have to." "Who wants to go to a stupid ballet?" I simply reminded him that his financial future squarely rested on his decision, and since he had no other source of revenue, I knew I was in control. That evening, kicking and screaming, he attended his first ballet performance. In summary, it was a very uncomfortable and disruptive evening for all of us. I don't know how, but we did get through the first season. The second season of the ballet was easier since there was less resistance, fewer complaints, and at least a neutral attitude. By the time the third season came around, there was no resistance at all. He dressed for the evening's activity without a verbal battle, and the conversation driving to the event was a typical parent-child conversation. On the way home I asked what he thought about the performance and was shocked by a comment I never expected to hear. "You know, dad," he began, "the company really has improved this year, hasn't it?" I knew by his question that it was no longer necessary to require him to attend the ballet. Our child was more comfortable with the environment and had developed some knowledge of the ballet. He would never be uncomfortable if the ballet might come up in a future discussion. Whether he ever attended another ballet again would be a decision he would make on his own. We, as parents, had done our job by giving him the exposure. Parental decision about lifestyle exposure situations are made in the areas of school, summer camp, sports activities, vacation, holiday plans, music involvement, dining experiences, and other areas that will affect their lives in later years. The more exposure to lifestyle experiences we give our children, the more we have empowered them by offering additional choices they will have throughout their lives.

Understanding Your Work, Community, and World Environments

One of the most practical uses of one's knowledge of the rules is to better understand the every day dynamics happening in the workplace and what we learn in the news. Knowing the rules allows you to better understand some of the reasons why one junior executive makes it to the senior ranks faster than another, when both seem to be doing equally effective and produce highly satisfactory work. It will also allow you to go beyond the headlines when leaders make domestic and international decisions. As mentioned before, for example, the rate Image (30%) and Exposure (60%) had on the results of the Kennedy/Nixon presidential debates. Those who heard the debates on the radio clearly claimed Nixon the winner from a Performance (10%) perspective. The vast number of Americans, however, saw the debates on television and witnessed Nixon in a gray suit against a gray background versus Kennedy in a rich blue suit that made him stand out in front of the same background. In addition, Nixon refused to be made up for the cameras and was sweating profusely, compared to a very cool looking John Kennedy under the same pressure of the debate. It was the image that carried the event and was a major factor in Kennedy defeating Nixon in the election.

Many times, a major political appointment can be explained by the rules. It is no accident that a Kennedy appointed his brain trust and inner circle from his New England associates. President Carter tapped into his known Georgia associates when he took office. There were probably many candidates who were more knowledgeable; however, there is always the need to surround oneself with the people you have worked with previously. Exposure and trust often outweigh performance.

Rules in the workplace can affect your life and career more profoundly on a daily basis. With knowledge of your organization's rules, you can make important decisions about dress, career planning (what job experiences will take you to the senior executive position of choice), choosing power networks, gaining sponsorship, getting promoted, and even maintaining and/or increasing job effectiveness. Many of the decisions you must make to be competitive are not always obvious. Organizational dynamics are often very subtle. The rules are overlooked mainly because we don't want to accept the realities of what we have observed. What we see going on might go against our personal value system, and we conclude what we are witnessing is wrong and will change over time. As a result, we don't make reality decisions but instead base our career decision on the utopia world we would like to see. You might have heard the statement, "It's not necessarily what you do around here, it's really who you know that counts." In this case, the person has observed the influence of exposure in the environment, but because of a "hard work" value system, feels this is wrong and eventually will be chosen for hard work and not their "networking" skills. The harsh reality is that this is just the rule and more than likely will never change. If that individual wants to remain competitive, they must alter their strategy and have the people who can make their career objectives happen get to know them and their capabilities better. To take this challenge on or not is simply a choice on the game board.

A Message to Our Young People

I know all this talk about rules and playing the game might lead you to want to stay young for as long as you possibly can. It sounds like it is restrictive, controlling, and not much fun. On the contrary, it is like most competitive games you play such as basketball, softball, golf, or tennis. Even though you have to work hard to achieve a competitive level of play, once you find that you can compete and even win, the game can be not only fun but also consuming. At this level, even the hard practice sessions are ones to which you look forward. This is probably due to the fact you feel you are getting better and will eventually compete even more successfully.

As it relates to being restrictive, learning to play the game of life actually gives you more freedom. Remember, we are suggesting that the game of life is made up of a series of choices. The more effectively you play the game, the more options or choices you open up for yourself. Make the choice to go to college instead of ending your formal education after completing high school and you have increased your choices for a career many fold; make the choice of getting good grades and you have expanded your choice of where you would like to go to college or eventually work. Just as playing by the rules of your athletic coach allows you to play the sport you like, playing by the rules of the game of life allows you to live and do the things you have always dreamed of doing. This is important to know when you are young. I realize that many young people have no idea of what they want to do or accomplish later in life. I know at twenty-four years of age, I didn't have a clue and had very few friends that weren't in the same place. It might be wonderful to have your life objectives clearly spelled out by the time you are fifteen years old, but few are fortunate enough to do so. A valid point to consider, however, is if you don't know now what you want to do, why not prepare yourself for as many options as possible? Furthering your education, learning new skills, and experiencing new environments all will expand your choices later in life.

You Are in the Game Already

Although Mom and Dad won't give you one hundred percent control over your choices, you nevertheless are very much in the game already. The game of life is very much like the experiences you are living in high school or college. Let's make a quick comparison. Your classroom teacher is very similar to a boss at work. They both have the right to make the rules in their environments and will grade you upon the results you produce. With work, doing a good job might allow you to keep your job, but it will not gain you a promotion. The same is true with your grades in school. To be considered by the good colleges, having good grades are just the minimum at which the college selection committee reviews. Were you involved in student government? Did you participate in extra-curricular activities? Can you get a good reference from your teachers not only for the academic work but also for conduct and attitude? All of these areas will be considered when it comes time to plan on college. Remember, there are many students that study hard and achieve good grades—this is a most important thing to do, but since it is the minimum level of acceptability it equates to ten percent weighing of performance on a job.

If you have ever interviewed for a summer job, I'm sure you have been told how to dress for that interview. Just as in later life, the interview gets you Exposure (60%) to a person that can make a difference in your life, and your Image (30%) will be a deciding factor of whether you get the job or not. Remember, most interviews are determined in the first twenty seconds as to your acceptability, and usually there are others who want the job as badly as you do. This scenario is exactly what you will be doing for the rest of your life. It will always be your choice, as it is now, as to the level of competitiveness you are willing to play in any game. Always read the environment in which you want to compete, decide how badly you want to be successful in that environment, and then make the choices that will allow it to happen. You are in total control of your choices. Remember, just like those who participate in sports, those who practice the hardest (in business we call it "paying dues") usually are the ones that make the first team. That is assuming they have the right attitude and follow the coach's rules.

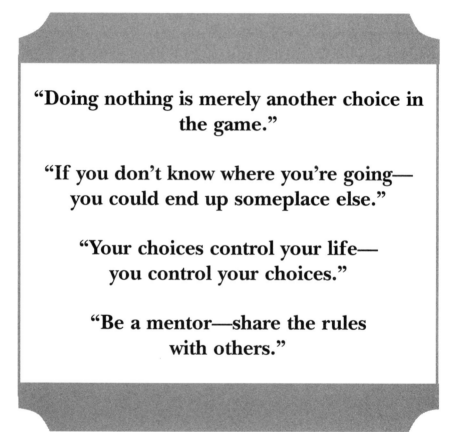

"Doing nothing is merely another choice in the game."

"If you don't know where you're going—you could end up someplace else."

"Your choices control your life—you control your choices."

"Be a mentor—share the rules with others."

CHAPTER 9

How to Learn the Rules of Your Organization

Since many of the rules are both unwritten and subtle, it is important to put some extra work in determining what the rules are in the environment in which you have chosen to play. In reading any new environment, whether it is work, school, social, religious, extra-circular activities, etc., it is important to observe, question, interpret, and then empower yourself to make the choices with which you can live.

The Skills of Reading the Environment

Professionals generally agree on the importance of reading and adapting to business environments. It is called survival! Those who do not accurately read and adapt to their environments usually come across as crude, uninformed, and lacking savvy—three bullets that can mortally wound any career or any sale.

The following pages outline a three-step process of reading an environment: *Observe, Question,* and *Interpret.* Even though *Adaptation* may be the ultimate agent of business success, accurate reading of the environment is the precursor of adaptation. Mastering this process will greatly enhance your knowledge and thus your ability to adapt, therefore, your ability to succeed.

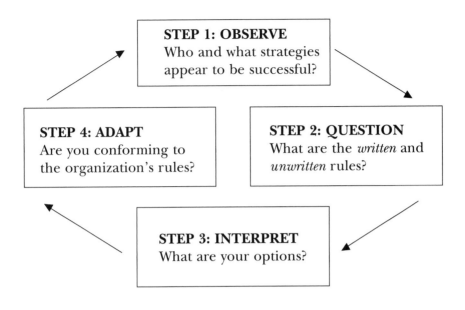

Step 1: Observe

Keen skills of observation are at the heart of reading any environment, whether it is in your organization or that of your customer. Watch everything and everyone. Go beyond the obvious and look for subtle messages and behaviors.

Your Immediate Sponsor (manager or potential customer): Observe behaviors and mannerisms of your immediate sponsor, and whenever possible, of potential sponsors above him or her.

- Is the general style open and informal or traditional and formal?
- Is the style of interaction rigid with hints of military protocol?
- Does communication style appear to shift with interaction between people of different levels within the organization?

- Is your sponsor comfortable communicating with his/her subordinates?
- Who strikes fear in the hearts of the masses?
- Who appears to be respected by most?
- Is your sponsor really a peer to others at his/her level, or does genuine influence elude him/her?
- What is the general image in attitude, appearance, and grooming at all levels?

Peers: Observe your peers as often as possible.

- Do your contacts seem to work as a team or independently?
- Is communication among your contacts free flowing or somewhat formal?
- Who appears to have the ear of upper management?
- Who do others seek out for advice and assistance?
- How does your sponsor interact with their subordinates and/or support staff?
- Does their general image mirror that of upper management? If not, what and where is the variation?

Levels Below Where You Interact: Observe the behaviors and mannerisms of persons at levels beneath your sponsor, whether it's your boss or your customer sponsor.

- Are they comfortable in approaching upper management?
- Do informal department and company social functions normally include or exclude these individuals?

- Who appears to have influence, not only within the group, but with upper management as well?
- What is the general image in attitude, appearance, and grooming?

Study written materials produced by the organization.

Is the general writing style used in letters and memos formal or conversational?

- What is the normal length of a letter or memo?
- Who gets copied and when?
- What are the department/organization or company "buzz words" used in most correspondence?

Observe the level of commitment the organization has to the community as demonstrated through support of: arts, education, and non-profit service organizations.

The key to gathering helpful data is to keep your antenna up at all times. Organizational dynamics are constantly changing. Do not be lulled into thinking, "It's always the same around here"—it rarely is.

Step 2: Question

Getting clarification of things you have observed will often require asking questions of others. It is essential to understand how, whom, and when to ask a question.

- Gain entrance into a network of information sharers. Mutual trust, respect, and common interests predicate this. The ability to quickly develop people linkages is key. Be open, flexible, and willing to make sacrifices that allow you to join in group activities. Allow others the opportunity to know you, the person, not just you, the professional. Once entrance into a network has been achieved, you will be part of open discussions about people and events, thereby, having many of your questions answered without asking.

- Always have definite reasons for asking a question. While it is not always necessary to verbalize your primary reasons, be prepared to offer at least a secondary explanation. Such an explanation should be given *before* asking the question. This strategy will minimize the "Why do you ask?" response.

- Be specific. This requires thinking through what you want to know before you ask the question. The more specific the question, the more likely you are to get a specific response.

- Be sensitive to the fact that your question may make the other person uncomfortable. Know when to back off. Perhaps answering your question will mean betraying a confidence—or that the level of trust is not sufficient for certain data to be shared. Carefully read any hesitation by the person of whom you asked the question. If it becomes clear the person is not simply thinking about your question, but seems reluctant to respond, you may then:

  —apologize for any uneasiness the question may have caused,

  —tell the person you understand a "no comment" response,

  —move on, changing the subject of the conversation.

Demonstrating this kind of sensitivity will often put this person at ease, allowing him/her to at least share some peripheral data.

- Be patient. Many times, questions can be answered by continuing to observe the situation. Delay asking questions until answers are no longer provided through observation.
- Be discrete. Never put anyone on the spot by asking sensitive questions in the presence of others. When in doubt about the sensitivity of any questions, don't ask! Wait for a more appropriate time and place.
- A final word about questioning. Any information gathered through questioning should be held as confidential. No amount of apologizing will restore enough trust to allow continued information sharing if a confidence is violated.

Step 3: Intrepret

Interpretation is the final step in reading any organization's environment, and is perhaps the toughest. It is as if there are several jigsaw puzzles being completed simultaneously. Pieces appear to fit one puzzle but belong to another. Although many assorted pieces are provided as you begin to observe and question, you must now fit the pieces together correctly for them to have any value.

- Know what you want from the environment. Interpretation is most relevant when it allows you to determine blocks and boosters. *Blockers* represent any persons or circumstances that may stop you from getting what you want. *Boosters* help you achieve objectives.

- Determine the cost of boosters. Nothing is free, and "there is always a price to pay." To gain a booster, the cost may include: working longer hours, imposing on time spent with family or friends, changing your basic communication style (verbal or non-verbal), socializing/ entertaining for business reasons, continuing your education leading to an additional degree, or relocation.

- Decide which boosters you are willing to pay for and which have too high a cost.

- Study the boosters that you feel cost too much (those for which you are unwilling to make sacrifices). Determine the career ramifications of not buying in. Specifically, as you have observed and questioned, what might have happened to others who did not "buy-in?"

- List all blockers. Determine who and what are the inherent blockers in the organization and which ones you can neutralize or turn into a booster. Blockers are most often found in the philosophy and mission of an organization. Is there opportunity for the realization of your goals, given the purpose, direction, and underlying philosophy of the organization? If the two are at odds with each other, you are facing a systemic blocker. Unlike other blockers, systemic blockers are just part of the system and are virtually immovable. If a blocker is not systemic, it can usually be at least neutralized. Most non-systemic blockers can be lumped into three separate groups: people, procedures, and you.

- Determine what it takes to neutralize a non-systemic blocker and decide if you are willing to take that on. The first step is to control your reaction to the blocker. Intensify observing and questioning to uncover a point or points of vulnerability.

- As with a booster, determine the business or career ramifications of not neutralizing a non-systemic blocker. Further, if you are confronting an inherent blocker, and you are unwilling to change, prepare for constant conflict. Recognize when your chances of winning these situations are less than slim and make additional choices that will minimize your losses. In extreme cases, this choice might be to simply move on to another environment that is more friendly and supportive.

Step 4: Adapt

After interpreting all the facts in any given situation, it finally boils down to making choices, evaluating one's commitment to the choices made, and more than likely requiring some changing on your part. These changes can be as simple as changing an attitude or changing something about your appearance or personality; or it can be as dramatic as changing your organization. Whatever it might be, the true impact of what you have learned in reading your environment lies in your ability to adapt to your new data. Remember, this game of life is based not on theory but on execution. Effective execution is normally connected to the degree of commitment that one is willing to apply to the situation. In that light, one should remain open, flexible, and always willing to adapt new perspectives and solutions to any situation. It is with adapting that players of the game can be and remain successful.

Make Choices That Make Sense for You

This is when the game gets personal, and no one can make the decisions for you that will define your life except you. That is not to say that many people do not allow others to define and direct their lives and careers. However, you are the person who will mainly have to live with your choices. All of us should listen to advice (it might allow us to make better choices), but to be empowered, all choices should be made by the person who must live out the ultimate decision.

The key to gaining greater control of your choices is to decide the major goals of your life. When you know what you want to accomplish, the smaller decisions you must make to get to those goals are clear and not difficult to make. If your goals are not defined, then any suggestions that others make will make sense. In reality, however, you will be living out the goals of others.

With Choices, You Are on Your Own—Have Fun!

CHAPTER 10

The Challenge

What Is Success?

As we mentioned, success in any organization covers a variety of options and isn't the same for everyone. From making a contribution in the same job for an entire career, to climbing the technical ladder, to becoming the person who runs the organization, to being a successful entrepreneur—all are meaningful areas that people choose as goals for business success. The key to personal success is setting goals that fit our personal values and lifestyle objectives. When any of those goals are accomplished, that individual will truly be successful.

The two most successful people I've ever known were my father and mother. My father died shortly after retirement from a cooking career and operating a catering business. My mother was a homemaker at first and then helped my father after their four children grew up. My father had a third grade education, and my mother reached the tenth grade in a farming community in Virginia. Their sole objective in life was to provide for their family and ensure their children got the very best start in life they could afford. This was not limited to possessions, but included strong values such as hard work, respecting other people, respecting yourself, and above all knowing that you could do whatever you set out to do. I think these days we refer to these messages as "good old family values." The one thing they were committed to was ensuring that all their children received a college education. At one time, three of us were in college at the same time, which required long hours and hard work from both of them. They pulled it off with style, grace, and love. All four of us have pursued successful careers in business, engineering, science, and medicine. Our success is a testament to them and their success.

I once asked my mother, if she had to do it all over again, would she change anything. I received a resounding "NO. Nothing!" She was happy, content, and as I said before, the most successful person I know. She and Dad had a goal, and they reached it. I know that story has been duplicated many times all over the world, but I'm just grateful that I was a part of their success.

The skills identified in this chapter are necessary to achieve your desired goals. Concerted effort, energy, and fine-tuning are required to maintain a high level of efficiency. Success does not happen overnight or by magic. However, with the consistent use of skills and a strong desire, it is possible for all of us to succeed.

Working in a Diverse World

With more and more people entering the workforce (and onto our teams) managers are urgently seeking ways to unite members of their units to make them more productive. This effort is called managing and valuing diversity. You have probably heard that for the next several decades we will experience one of the most diverse workforce and customer sets in the history of this country. You may already see some of these changes in your industry, organization, or immediate work unit. The increase in women, minorities, foreign born, older workers, gays, lesbians, and disabled workers has already become a reality in many cities, industries, and organizations. This diversity could be the most powerful tool we carry into the game. It will give us new energy, new perspectives, and new solutions, *if* we maximize everyone's potential. In order for this to happen, however, we must learn to effectively work together.

For teams to be effective, team members must talk and listen to each other, value each other's uniqueness, respect and trust each other, show a desire for the team to be successful, be willing to give up some individual things for the good of the whole team, be willing to take personal responsibility or ownership for their actions, and always do their personal best. We can see by some of these requirements that a diverse workforce may have much more difficulty accomplishing effective teamwork than people with common backgrounds and values.

Success Does Not Happen in a Vacuum

Remember, this is a people game. You cannot be successful without people. That is why you can only be as successful as those who support you inside and outside of the organization.

Some of the major barriers to a smoothly operating team include: mistrust, suspicion, misunderstandings, lack of communication, not feeling included, and not feeling empowered. If these conditions exist, the organization and/or manager can experience: drop in quality, a disruptive workforce with constant peer/peer and employee/manager misunderstandings, high employee turnover, increased absenteeism and tardiness, a rise in discrimination charges, employee complaints, and the formation of angry internal support groups. Any, if not all, of these can result in a drop in overall productivity.

Internal support groups are increasing within organizations. This occurs when various factions within the organization form a group among teammates who share common backgrounds and common values. These common perspectives could be based on gender, race, ethnic backgrounds, age, sexual orientation, and so on. Normally, the purpose of these groups is very positive. They want to talk with other people about the business culture that understands their perspective, challenges, and frustrations. They want to give feedback to the organization as to how the culture might change to become more effective for them and their group members. In addition, members of the groups want to learn more about the rules of the system and don't know where to find that information. They want to mentor young people of their group and teach them what they need to know early in their careers to give them a better chance for success.

The negative impact of these groups is that they highlight the lack of trust between them and the organization. This movement is similar to the rise of unions in this country, when people felt that the only way they could be heard was by uniting. Then, as well as now, there is an obvious breakdown in the organization's support and communication channels. Not until managers and team members take on the responsibility of mentoring and growing others, will trust re-enter our workforce. Without a doubt, the most powerful tool managers have to help motivate people and to shorten the trust gap is to help employees grow. By teaching people the "rules," they know you care and have less need to seek information through internal support groups.

Progressive organizations are aggressively altering their cultures to better meet the realities and challenges of today's workforce. Day care centers, flexible work hours, shared jobs, work at home opportunities, and even changing to casual attire are all attempts to make individuals more productive.

One of the major cultural changes, in many organizations, is to empower employees. This is an attempt to give employees more control over their work areas and their careers. These efforts should be applauded but will not be totally effective if people don't know the rules of the game that they are playing. In essence, no one can be in control if the rules have not been taught.

Leaders who share the game rules with their employees set up a common standard for the entire team. When everyone knows what it takes to succeed, suspicion, mistrust, and cries of favoritism fade quickly. Teammates will know why certain employees are moved ahead and what they must do to be among the chosen. Without this information, most people who are working hard for advancement will react with a feeling that the leader and organization doesn't really care about their progress, but only want what they can get from the individual and then they will be discarded. It is very hard to build a trusting, motivating environment when people don't know the formula necessary to be effective in their jobs or how to move their careers ahead.

(Again) Knowledge Is Power

It is easy for individuals who did not grow up in mainstream America to feel that they are victims of the system. If you don't understand the system, you feel powerless to do things for yourself. You wait for management to move your career, when they feel you are ready. For those leaders who only talk about performance, it is easy for employees to conclude that it is the sole criteria for advancement. They will build their psychological contract on the fact that if they become the performer you want them to be, you will honor their desire to move higher in the organization. When this movement doesn't happen, most likely your once trusting relationship will be destroyed.

The solution for this dilemma is very clear both for organizations and individual relationships: Share all of the rules of the game with everyone.

But the Game Isn't Fair!

We've talked about that statement before, as well as with the comment, "It's not easy either." Both statements are accurate. Of course, if the game was easy, every person or company would be at or near the top of the pyramid in which they play. To ensure that only a few reside at the top, the dynamics there are fast-paced and filled with risk. To survive, one must be competitive, energetic, tough-minded, focused, and willing to pay dues and put in time.

The fairness of the game is translated through the eyes of the beholder. All will not see or evaluate the rules the same way and in many cases with just cause. For example, is it fair for a non-English speaking person to "play the game" in the United States where he/she must speak English? Or for women to have to participate in game activities that are traditionally male oriented, like golf, or to expect Asian, African, and Hispanic Americans to play by a set of rules that were created by European Americans? How about being disabled, or sick, or poor, or even too short, or too tall? I'm afraid the list could go on and on. It is fair to say that it would be impossible to create a set of rules that would allow everyone to think the game was truly "fair" for all. The best the game can do is to allow everyone, who wishes, to compete and be judged by their ability to execute according to the rules. This execution might be at the expense of overcoming challenges other players may never face.

Franklin D. Roosevelt became president of the United States despite the fact that he had polio and was unable to walk without assistance; Colin Powell became joint chiefs of staff and then secretary of state, despite the fact that his parents were not from European ancestry; John D. Rockefeller became a billionaire despite coming from working class parents; Henry Kissinger became secretary of state despite the fact that he came from a non-English speaking family; and Janet Reno became attorney general of the United States despite the fact that she is not male. All of these people had a strong case showing that the game wasn't fair for them because each of them had to overcome something extra which their competitor did not have to contend. That challenge did not stop any of them. By tapping into their talents and skills and executing the rules, they were able to finish on top of their respective pyramids. That is about as fair as it will ever get!

Another example of how the game allows all to play according to their ability can be seen on the global scene. In the 1980s and early 1990s the Japanese once owned the top thirteen banks in the world. If the game was controlled or "rigged" by Europeans, do you really think they would have allowed the Japanese to dominate the world financial market? Of course not! The simple fact is that the Japanese learned the rules and executed them better than everyone else.

Think Outside of the Box

The one thing of which we can be assured in playing the game is that it will not always be easy. There will always be obstacles, problems, challenges, setbacks, defeats, and situations where you will feel cornered. These are the testing times—the times when you will be forced to determine not only how important it is for you to reach your objective but be tested if your creative skills can help get you back on track. Many believe (as well as I) that there is a solution to every challenge as long as you are willing to take some risks and pay a price. Each of us must answer the question, "Is it worth the price I have to pay?" Once you think of a solution to a problem, determine if it is the right solution for you and/or if your goals are still important.

Often, to come up with the most effective solutions you must think outside of the box. There is a tendency to apply solutions that have approaches you have always used, ones that are known and comfortable. But as we well know, what worked once may not be the right answer every time. Some situations require a departure from your comfort zone and possibly a need to take some risks. Thinking outside of our norms usually makes us feel uncomfortable or vulnerable, but often this is exactly what the situation requires. During this creative process, you need to remain flexible while reviewing all solutions, particularly new ones. Don't reject new thoughts and ideas until you've had a chance to thoroughly investigate all angles.

Be a good listener, because the perfect solution can come from a person in any conversation. Be ready for it by listening to what people tell you. Don't get bogged down in emotion, it can stop the creative process faster than anything else. Finally, start to think differently. Great discoveries may occur by thinking 180 degrees from your current direction. For example, the cure for polio came from the polio virus itself! To save space, someone concluded that to wash a car, why pull the car through the brushes? Instead, why not let the car remain stationary and let the brushes do the moving?

What thinking opposite will allow you to do is to open your mind to all possibilities. Maybe the best answer is only 90 degrees from your first thought, but by thinking outside the box you have a good chance of finding the right solution. Remember, there is a solution to every problem, and our job is to find it!

Remember: You Are in Control

Sometimes when everything seems to be going wrong, it's hard to convince ourselves that we are in control. After all, logic says that if I controlled my situation I wouldn't put myself through so much pain and agony. Although you cannot foresee or eliminate all of the challenges that lie ahead, through the skills of planning, emotional control, creative problem solving, being able to connect with people (who can help), and through risk taking, we can lighten and even avoid future problems by taking control of ourselves in the game. Even when unavoidable crises hit, our choices determine how long we will stay in those crises. It all comes down to personal choices, and only we make them in and for our lives.

Set the Right Goals

One of the reasons we linger in problem situations longer than we want is simply because we are not sure of where we want to go. When we are truly committed to making something happen or to accomplishing a goal, nothing stands in our way. When a person has an inspirational commitment to reaching a goal, many of the problems encountered along the way are viewed as trivial or just a nuisance. The problems still must be resolved, but they are viewed as insignificant when compared to the overall objective or goal. Without a vision or goals, problems are the focus, they take center stage, and are all consuming. Once you get bogged in the detail and emotion of a problem, you forget the goals you have set, and the problem very easily becomes the goal. If you lose sight of *why* you want to solve any problem, you stop trying. This leads to complacency and eventually feeling like a victim. The "poor me" attitude is a sign that someone has given up control. To prevent this, set goals for your life. Decide what you want, where you want to go, and what it will take to get there. Make sure you decide on goals that are *yours* and not someone else's. Only *you* can motivate *you* to do the things necessary to make it happen. It is not advisable to put one hundred percent effort into achieving someone else's goals.

A final thought is one that I know you have heard before, but it's worth repeating. Have some fun! Remember, life is not a destination, it is a journey—it's what you experience along the way!

Just Do It!

We have spent an entire book outlining the rules of the game. Obviously, knowing the rules are important, but like any game it comes down to **execution**—not just talking about it. The sports team that has the best game plan but does not execute it favorably will lose. The business that has a great strategic plan but doesn't execute the plan will go out of business. A similar fate awaits our career and life plans if we don't execute. The question we need to ask ourselves is, "When is what I do good enough?" Well, to a large extent that depends on your competition. If your competitors are weak, you might not have to go "all out" to stay ahead of them. However, if your competitors are sharp and want the prize badly enough, you must be at your very best. I believe in those intense competitive battles (which can also be a lot of fun) are the times when we are pushed and forced to go beyond normal achievement. Just as "without competition we cannot have excellence" is true for organizations, it is also true that without competition we cannot grow to our maximum potential. Competition brings out the best and worst in all of us, but if we are in an improvement frame of mind it always makes us stronger.

In these situations, try to not execute *only* the big and important things. Winners are usually the ones who have paid attention to the little things. In 2001 Tiger Woods finished the PGA tour as the number one money winner. It was determined that number thirty-five on the list, Jerry Kelly, averaged only $1^1/_2$ strokes per 18 holes less than Tiger Woods. The little things Tiger Woods was doing placed him thirty-four spots ahead of Jerry Kelly on the money list. These become the differences that win competitive situations.

Never Stop Growing

People who succeed in their careers and in the game of life never stop learning. Many of us in our formal education years felt that if we could just get out of school, we would never have to go through the learning process ever again. As we get older, we constantly identify all the things we wish we had learned when we were younger. The fact is, real learning never stops. I'm told that when, at ninety-four, Pablo Casals was playing one of his final concerts at the Kennedy Center in Washington, D.C., and he was asked why he still practiced four hours a day, his response was simply, "I think I'm making progress." I think with that attitude, it is impossible *not* to succeed. Remember, the race is not over until it is over! Once you know what you want, keep on growing, continue learning, never give up, and understand that you can't do it alone. No matter what your objectives, it takes people to help you get there and to help you enjoy the victories after you have achieved them.

Success is how *you* define it and the choices *you* make to achieve it. *You* are as empowered as *you* want to be. *You* are in control.

Have a good game!

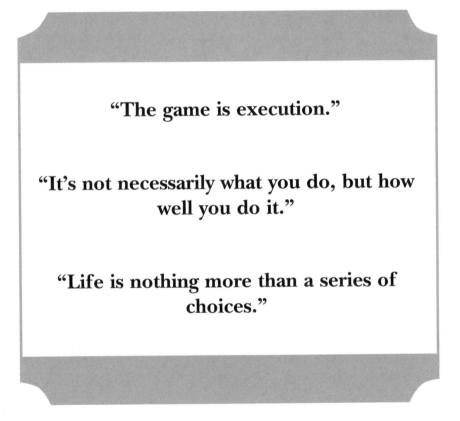

"The game is execution."

"It's not necessarily what you do, but how well you do it."

"Life is nothing more than a series of choices."